AN INVALUABLE RESOURCE THAT OFFERS SUPPORT AND PROVEN
SOLUTIONS FOR ANY PARENT FACING THE CHALLENGE OF
LOVING EACH ONE BEST

"Nancy Samalin has done it again. She has combined wisdom, humor, and a
heavy dose of practical advice to all parents who find themselves dealing
with the onslaught of sibling competition."

—Lawrence Balter, Ph.D., author of *Not in Front of the Children: How to
Talk to Your Child About Tough Family Matters*

"Ms. Samalin's experience, wisdom, and practicality are best captured in the
voices of real parents from her workshops, which give this excellent book a
truly authentic quality."

—Stanley Turecki, M.D., author of *The Difficult Child* and *Normal Children
Have Problems, Too*

"Nancy brings the silent thoughts and feelings we all share into the
light by giving voice to them so we can understand ourselves and love
our children better."

—Vicki Lansky, author of *Practical Parenting Tips*

"There's little that drives a household more dramatically than the sibling
dynamic—a subject so formidable few have had the courage to tackle it.
Nancy Samalin uses her incredible experience and willingness to learn in
this wonderful book. It should be handed out as required reading when we
leave the hospital with number two."

—Dr. Ron Taffel, author of *Parenting by Heart* and *Why Parents
Disagree . . . and What You Can Do About It*

NANCY SAMALIN

with Catherine Whitney

Loving
Each One Best

A Caring and Practical
Approach to Raising Siblings

BANTAM BOOKS
NEW YORK   TORONTO   LONDON   SYDNEY   AUCKLAND

LOVING EACH ONE BEST
PUBLISHING HISTORY
Bantam hardcover edition published February 1996
Bantam trade paperback edition / February 1997

ISBN 0-553-37834-1

Published simultaneously in the United States and Canada

*Bantam Books are published by Bantam Books, a division of Bantam Doubleday Dell Publishing
Group, Inc. Its trademark, consisting of the words "Bantam Books" and the portrayal of a rooster, is
Registered in U.S. Patent and Trademark Office and in other countries. Marca Registrada. Bantam
Books, 1540 Broadway, New York, New York 10036.*

PRINTED IN THE UNITED STATES OF AMERICA

FFG   10   9   8   7   6   5   4   3   2   1

To Sy,

*Who for more than three decades
has continued to enrich my life with his
unconditional love and warmth.*

and to Eric and Todd,

*Who have been our best teachers of the joys and
challenges of sibling relationships. Their love and
respect for one another unite our family, reminding
us daily of all the best reasons
to have more than one.*

Acknowledgments

My special thanks to the real experts, the parents themselves. I am especially grateful to those in my workshops, some of whom have been with me for many years. I hope they know the extent to which their insights, openness, and enthusiasm have sustained and inspired me. In addition to my workshop participants, I am grateful to all the parents who took the time from their busy lives to fill out my eight-page questionnaire. Without the generosity of these parents and their willingness to share their ideas, this book would not be such a solid resource for other caring, struggling parents. Although you know who you are, I wish I could thank each one of you personally.

I have been very lucky to have the guidance of Wendy McCurdy, an inspired editor whose personal as well as professional expertise has nourished this book. Wendy's passionate advocacy for these ideas stems from her own parenting experiences and from her skill and sensitivity as an editor.

I am indebted to Catherine Whitney, a gifted writer who has earned my respect and gratitude for her clarity, enormous patience, and flexibility. It is a pleasure and a privilege to work with her.

My literary agent, Jane Dystel, has gone out of her way to be available for me when I need her, no matter how busy she is. I appreciate both her professionalism and her in-depth knowledge of publishing.

The following people accepted the arduous task of reading and advising me on the manuscript, a most generous use of their valuable time. They are Ann Banks, Zel Hopson, Patricia McCormick, Todd Samalin, Dr. Ron Taffel, and Julie Walsh.

I am delighted to be associated with Ann Pleshette Murphy, editor in chief of *Parents*. I consider it a privilege to be a contributing editor to a magazine truly dedicated to the well-being of families. The executive editor at *Parents*, Wendy Schuman, was not only the catalyst for this project, she has also been supportive of my work for many years. Her encouragement has meant a lot to me. Thanks are also due to Lou Aronica, who originated the idea for this book.

I am most grateful to Marty Edelston, who invited me to join the panel of experts at his excellent magazine, *Bottom Line\Personal* as well as to his talented senior editor, Marc Myers.

I deeply appreciate the support of the following people: Barbara and Don Coloroso of Kids Are Worth It, Jim Trelease of Reading Tree Productions, and Dr. Larry Kutner of Harvard Medical School. They are gifted speakers and authors who have been exceptionally generous and helpful with their time and advice.

Among the many other professionals I have worked with who deserve a special note of thanks are: Marcia Burch at Penguin USA, along with Debbie Yautz and Jean Arlotta; Arlynn Greenbaum of Authors Unlimited; Zel Hopson at the Nanaimo Family Life Association; Sandra Levy at SSA; Hal Morgan at Work/Family Directions; Suellen Newman and her students at the Hudson School; Larry Rood and Leah Curry Rood and their helpful staff at Gryphon House; Bob Wolf and all the talented people at Chiat/Day, including Dave Butler and Fred Rubin; and Eileen Wasow, associate dean at Bank Street College of Education.

Janet Schuler and Al Fariello were a big help in researching, organizing, and transcribing material for this book. My thanks as well to Jane Harrison and Maria Pereira, who so graciously hosted several series of parent workshops in their homes.

I am blessed with many friends and colleagues who have made a special difference in my life and work. In particular, I would like to express my appreciation to Dr. Lawrence Balter, Arlette Brauer, Linda

Braun, Ann Caron, Elizabeth Crary, Susan Ginsberg, Barbara Hemphill, Ruth Hersh, Joan and James Levine, Andrea Kiernan, Vicki Lansky, Stephania McClennen, Florence Mitchell, Dr. Ildiko Mohacsy, Dr. Alvin Rosenfeld, Judy Snyder, Jean Soichet, Mary Solow, Lydia Spinelli, Dr. Ron Taffel, Marvin Terban, Len and Marilyn Weinstock, and Ira Wolfman.

And, of course, my deepest appreciation to my family, who mean so much to me: my mother, Liz Kaufmann, whose positive attitude and capacity for enjoying life have kept her incredibly young and vigorous, as well as providing me with an inspiring role model; my stepmother, Ruth Hettleman, a true believer in the value of education, who has been extremely generous and supportive of us and our sons. And to my sister, Ellen, and my brother, Tom, who have taught me so much about the joys and complexities of sibling relationships.

Finally, this book is written in loving memory of my brother, Tom Hettleman.

Contents

Loving
Each One Best

Chapter 1

From One to a Handful

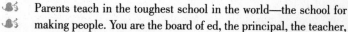

Parents teach in the toughest school in the world—the school for making people. You are the board of ed, the principal, the teacher, and the janitor all rolled into two . . . and there is no general agreement on the curriculum. You are on duty, or at least on call, 24 hours a day, 365 days a year, for at least 18 years for each child you have.

—Virginia Satir,
The New Peoplemaking

My son Eric was only three months old when I realized I might be pregnant again. My initial reaction was "I can't believe this is happening!" Full of apprehension, I made an appointment with my doctor for a pregnancy test.

But a funny thing happened in the doctor's office. When he told me that, yes, I was pregnant, instead of feeling despair, I was elated. I knew I had wanted two children, although I'd never expected them to be so close in age. Yet, suddenly it seemed like a great idea. Now we'd be more than just two adults and a child. We'd be a "whole" family. As I prepared for the arrival of my second child, I often found myself daydreaming about the way it would be, conjuring up heartwarming pictures of happy harmony. I imagined my children as loving companions, lifelong buddies who would grow up together, share secrets, develop fierce loyalties, be friends through thick and thin. The prospect brought me an intense antici-pation of pride and pleasure.

But as is so often the case, reality was very different from the rosy ideal. I was completely caught off guard by the challenge of raising two sons—the extra pressures, the exhaustion, the feeling that I had to mediate every argument, the fear that they would never love one an-other. I hated the shrill sound of my voice barking orders, nagging, pleading for peace. The harmonious world of my dreams was replaced by the war zone of our daily life together.

Of course, I blamed myself. Surely, if I had been a more competent parent, I would be able to instill in them the desire to be more loving toward one another, and teach them how to end their fighting and bickering. I spent a lot of time feeling inadequate, but had I only been more knowledgeable about the normal dynamics between brothers, I would have realized that rivalry, conflict, and competition were inevita-ble, and they could even be a healthy part of a sibling relationship.

Contrary to my worst fears, their childhood conflicts did not set Eric and Todd up for a lifetime of hard feelings. Just the opposite. My sons are young men now, and they have weathered their childhood rivalry quite cheerfully. None of my worst fears has come to pass. Better still, their lives have been immensely enriched by their relationship. Long before they reached adulthood, they had become each other's best friends and confidants, and they remain so today. Although they live in different cities, they speak almost daily on the phone. Their closeness gives me great joy. As I think back to those years when I worried so much, I can't believe how much energy I wasted.

Who Has Answers?

When I was approached to write a book about raising more than one child, my first reaction was "Are there really workable answers to all the problems and complexities within the sibling relationship?" And my second concern was "Do parents really want or need a book like this? Haven't they already been inundated with too much advice?" But as I began to talk to parents about the idea, I was astonished by the amount of passion they felt about this issue— and how eager they were to find practical, workable suggestions and new solutions to try.

Many parents were surprised and disappointed, as I had once been, that having that first child had not made them "experts" on being parents. Faced with their second, third, and fourth child, they still felt tremendous insecurity, and were very enthusiastic about the idea of a book that would address their concerns. I heard again and again of their surprise that having many children, or even two children, was such a huge difference from having one, and how unprepared they felt to deal with it. They couldn't believe how much additional work it was to have more than one, how many more decisions there were to make, how complex and unique each child was.

Yet, as I began to see the urgent need for such a book, I felt troubled by the enormity of the task. I honestly wondered whether there *were* any real solutions to the chaos and stress of sibling demands and squabbling. What could I tell parents that would ease the load, give them practical tools, provide support and hope? I saw that people were searching for something more profound than simply a collection of "parenting tips." They were looking for *real* answers to concrete dilemmas. In every group of parents, as soon as I raised the issue of siblings, the floodgates opened. Deep feelings and admissions, previously unspoken, came pouring out:

- The mother who breast-fed her baby in secret because she feared her six-year-old daughter would feel jealous and abandoned.
- The mother who described in dismay how her formerly angelic young son was transformed into a "monster"—starting with the moment he pinched his newborn brother on the way home from the hospital.
- The working mom whose days and nights were such an ex-

hausted blur that she was losing the ability to find pleasure in her children.

- The father burdened by his "guilty secret"—that he loved his third child best.
- The mother of four who complained that the endless caretaking made her feel like a drudge—"Everyone else comes first, and there's nothing left for me," she reported wearily.
- The mother who was moved to tears when her son confessed, "I hate my sister. I hate her!"
- The father who couldn't believe his eyes when he found his four-year-old trying to strangle her two-year-old brother.
- The woman who grieved over the lost intimacy she had once shared with her firstborn.
- The father who admitted that since the arrival of his third child he worked extra-long hours to avoid the chaos at home.
- The parent who, as an only child herself, was horrified by the way her three children argued and fought.

There were moments of humor, too—albeit ironic humor:

- The mother who gradually lowered her expectations to the point where "My goal in life is five uninterrupted minutes in the bathroom."
- The couple who spent their seventh wedding anniversary eating a "romantic" candlelit dinner of leftover pizza after the kids were finally in bed.
- The woman who confessed, "My oldest was a poster child for the five food groups of nutritious eating. My third child—one of the first words out of his mouth was 'McDonald's.' "

But whether the words are spoken with humor or irony, the underlying message is the same: So many parents of more than one child admit to feeling pushed to the breaking point. Don't get me wrong. It's not that they don't experience enormous joy and satisfaction. I've rarely met a parent who regretted the decision to have more than one child. But often the satisfaction is blunted by feelings of frustration, disappoint-ment, exhaustion, and guilt. Parents are eager to know if they can change things, and if so, how.

"Did I Make the Right Decision?"

Many parents have described to me how they had agonized over the decision to have another child, weighed all the pros and cons, and finally decided that the best thing they could do for their first child was to give him a sibling. They were filled with the images of happy fam-ilies—the TV sitcom ideals and the fantasies they recalled from their youth. Many were disillusioned when their own families didn't even begin to measure up to their idealized goals. Frequently, they'd grown up in homes where spanking and yelling were the norm, and they vowed they would not repeat the mistakes their parents had made. But as one woman said sadly, "When I'm screaming at my kids, I hear my mother's voice in my own, and I can't believe it's really me. I was so much calmer and in control when it was just one child."

Time and again, parents have told me that the decision to have another child was made in the eager anticipation of making the family stronger, more loving, and more fun. I was surprised by the number of parents who said their families didn't seem quite "real" when there was only one child. But then, as the size of their families increased, instead of the warmth and happiness they had anticipated, they were often overwhelmed by a different reality: As the kids began avidly vying for attention, picking on each other, trading insults, and hitting, the par-ents reacted by becoming worn down, chronically irritated, and unable to intervene effectively.

I realized that these parents felt they had never really been heard by the "experts" whose advice columns filled newspapers and magazines and whose books lined the child-care sections of their local bookstores. They had read many books and articles about preparing older children for new babies or handling sibling rivalry, some of which made them feel more inadequate. "Usually the advice I read just adds to my guilt," said one mother. "There is so much pressure to be loving and sensitive and to always say the right thing. I can't identify with most of what I read. And when I'm stressed or exhausted, forget it. All the advice flies out the window."

It occurred to me that most advice about parenting is child centered. Little space is allowed for parents to express and work through their own "unacceptable" emotions. Often parents are given too little credit for the tremendous sacrifices they make. People without kids or those whose kids are grown don't appreciate just how difficult it is to be a good parent. It often seems when children do well, they get the credit—as they should. But when they misbehave, *you* get blamed. You can feel the disapproval—almost hear people thinking, *Why can't she control her children?*

I've often reflected on how much work, time, and extraordinary patience it takes to be a parent of even one child. And when two or three or more children enter the picture, the tolerance quotient gets stretched to the limit.

When you think about it, what is parenting but a denial of our own needs for the sake of those small (or not so small), demanding, ever-present beings who are in our care? To meet their needs, we often have to sacrifice our own. For example, children need to make a mess; we adults need order and neatness. Children require lots of attention; adults need periods of solitude. Children need noise; adults need quiet and tranquillity. Children need to dawdle, dream, explore, and ask endless questions; adults need to hurry, be organized, plan ahead, and get places on time. And so on. The reality of being a good parent usually involves a conflict of needs. That's what makes the job so tough.

Even so, parents rarely give themselves a break or acknowledge the enormity of their challenge. Instead, they worry constantly about whether they're doing a good enough job, and whether their kids will turn out all right, and what, if anything, they could be doing that would make a difference.

All parents struggle with guilt. But there are special issues and added layers that come with parenting more than one. I have found that many parents with two or more children look back longingly on the period before their second child was born, believing that their lives were saner, more controlled, and even happier then. On their worst days, they might wonder if they made the right choice when they decided to expand their families. Many people who felt competent parenting one child now find it's a completely new ball game requiring a whole separate set of techniques. "Where did my parenting skills go?" groaned one mother in frustration. "I used to think I was a wonderful mom."

I've met parents who were so hard on themselves that the first time they felt intense anger toward their children they wanted to turn themselves in to the Parenting Police. For instance, I've seen couples who had waited so long to have a child that they were amazed their kids could make them so enraged. They were shocked at their first flash of fury, or the first time their child shouted, "I hate you!"—as though their great love should have immunized them both against angry outbursts. I know a couple who waited six years to have their second child. Their reaction to the event was as one might expect: delight and wonder, immense elation, great jubilation. But when night after night the new baby refused to be comforted even after many hours of pacing the floor, while their first child reverted to making babylike demands of his own, these sleep-deprived parents felt resentful, frustrated, and desperate for time away from their children. I've heard parent after parent describe the joy and expectation of waiting for the birth of a second child, or a third, only to wonder in the chaotic aftermath if they had made the right decision. If only they knew that most parents have similar doubts, I am convinced it would ease their anxiety.

When my sons were young, I was always trying to prove to my mother that I was a terrific parent—indeed, a better parent than she had been. It was mostly subconscious, this desire to be seen as the perfect mother, and it always backfired. I would set the stage by expecting my children to behave in an exemplary way in front of my mother so that they would reflect positively on me. Not surprisingly, Todd and Eric picked up on my unarticulated wishes and refused to cooperate. (Kids seem to have a built-in radar for this kind of thing!) They were obnoxious around my mother. They were whiny. They were clingy. The harder I tried to get them to behave as model children, the more they rebelled. They sensed I was using them as puppets, wanting to show them off—and they weren't about to perform on cue.

It took many years before I began to realize how I had been trying to make my children reinforce my own sense of self-worth. And I wondered, why was I so anxious to appear like such an ideal mother? What was I trying to prove—and to whom was I trying to prove it? Well, for one thing, I was trying to prove what a great mother I was to my own mother. But I was also trying to prove it to myself because it was something I had great doubt about. I was sobered by the extent of my insecurity. And over the years, that insecurity has been a recurrent theme for many parents in my workshops and lecture audiences.

You're Not Alone

Perhaps the most important thing I have to offer in this book is the advice and wisdom of other parents. I have found, during my two decades of conducting workshops, that parents find the greatest support from each other. The mother who is overwhelmed by the demands of her household can begin to laugh about it when she hears another woman describe her similar plight with humor. A parent who feels compelled to intercede whenever her kids argue finds relief by listening to another mother who announces she's "kid deaf" to the squabbling. Parents who complain that they squeeze in "quality time" between the mountains of laundry, the pile of dishes in the sink, their eight-hour jobs, and the constantly interrupted phone calls are relieved to hear that other parents faced with the same dilemma find brief moments of satisfaction throughout the day instead of trying to set aside big chunks of "quality time".

Most often, the greatest wisdom available to harried parents comes from the mouths of other parents. Although what works for one family may not work for another, and what works for Michael may not work for Michelle, there's usually something worthwhile to try within the smorgasbord of creative ideas. We all benefit enormously from this sharing. No child comes equipped with instructions, but why should each new parent start from scratch and reinvent the wheel? There are no manuals for what to do when a second child enters the scene—or a third or fourth—but we can find aid, comfort, inspiration, and information in the experiences of others. And although this is not a book of "shoulds," or recipes for instant success, it is full of techniques and ideas that work to alleviate the added stresses that come with the expanding family. It's my chance to give readers access to the rich supply of insights supplied by the real experts—the parents themselves.

This book is the result of many workshops (including some with the kids themselves), speeches, seminars, and the responses of hundreds of parents of siblings throughout the country who dedicated time and reflection to answering a detailed questionnaire on their personal experiences of raising more than one. It will relieve many harried parents to learn that there truly are solutions to many of their concerns.

I believe this book will give you some new ideas, and also help you feel less isolated. Think of the voices in this book as your personal support group.

There's Hope!

The fact that you are reading this book already says you are a caring parent who wants to learn to be the best you can be. In spite of all the joy and satisfaction that come with having more than one child, all responsible parents struggle with exhaustion, guilt, frustration, and disappointment as well.

In the pages of this book, you'll find new ways to handle some of the more aggravating and mystifying aspects of raising more than one child—such as:

- How to cope with the arrival of the new baby whose entrance challenges your other children's sovereignty.

- Practical tips for easing the sheer pressure and stress of mornings, bedtimes, and the hours in between.
- How to carve out personal time for yourself without feeling guilty.
- Workable strategies for getting dads involved.
- Actual solutions for when kids fight, bicker, compete, name-call, and hit.
- How to be "fair" without having to treat them equally.
- How to find special time alone with each child, and to celebrate each one's uniqueness rather than lumping them together as "the kids."
- How to handle the inevitable angry moments without totally losing it.
- Where to find the humor in those trying moments when you need it the most.

One of the most gratifying things that happened when I was writing this book was that I began to see how parents really were successfully making changes. I was often impressed with the unexpected ways in which they coped, and the creative solutions they invented. And I was frequently moved by how much a simple word of encouragement or a suggestion between parents could make a real difference.

One afternoon around five o'clock (better known by parents as "the arsenic hour"), I took a break from my work to go to the supermarket. On the checkout line in front of me was a woman whose two small boys were fighting loudly over a toy. One grabbed it roughly as the other one screamed bloody murder. While everyone stared, their embarrassed mother desperately tried to quiet them. She gave me a miserable, apologetic look. I smiled at her and said, "I know just what you're going through. I went through the same thing when my boys were that age. There were times they would have liked to kill each other, but if it's any consolation, now that they're grown they would kill *for* each other."

The woman's face brightened. Letting her know I had been there too helped her feel less embarrassed and gave her some perspective during a trying moment. As I walked home from the supermarket I was struck by the fact that sometimes the most meaningful advice appears as if by magic in the odd moments when you least expect it. I knew what I had to do was to gather up all those moments and present them as a gift to parents of more than one child. The result is this book.

Chapter 2

Bringing Home Number Two

Look! You don't even have a lap anymore. That baby is taking up all the room, and it isn't even born yet.

—Martha Alexander,
When the New Baby Comes,
I'm Moving Out

Except for twins, every firstborn or first-adopted child is an *only* child for a time. The experience of parenting the first is unique, scary, precious—a new and dramatic adventure. It is the transformation from an adult-centered to a child-centered household. Many parents believe that once they have made the transition from having no children to having their first, the rest should be smooth sailing. But the arrival of a second child is a disruption with unique features all its own. Even after elaborate preparation, the introduction of a sibling can be a frustrating process—especially for your first child. After all, a young child who hears, "We're having another child because we love you so much," is not warmed by such a sentiment. To his way of thinking it's not that different from a husband who says to his wife, "I love you so much and I'm so happy with you that I want to double my joy. So I'm getting another wife. She may be a little younger and cuter, but you can share me, as well as all your favorite things, with her!"

Eric was only one year old when I brought Todd home from the hospital. To this day, I remember the scene. When I went to hug Eric, he stiffened and turned his face away from me. I was shocked by his reaction. I didn't see things through his eyes: Not only had I left him for a few days but I returned with someone else! He was not about to agree that we were doing something wonderful for him by presenting him with a baby brother. At the time, I couldn't understand how different this "blessed event" appeared from his perspective.

Kids are concrete thinkers. They see love as something to be measured out. They don't realize that the more you have, the more you have to give. To them, love is as finite as M&M's; if you give some away, there won't be as much left for them. So when a new baby is vying for your attention, they're likely to see the baby as an unwelcome interloper.

I doubt if there's an only child in existence who isn't shocked when his or her solitary reign ends. I love the story that the writer Anna Quindlen tells about how this realization dawned on her firstborn child when he wanted her attention and she couldn't oblige. She writes: "It began one day when the younger one needed me more, and I turned to my older son, Quin, and said, 'You know, Quin, I'm Christopher's mommy, too.' The look that passed over his face was the one that usually accompanies the discovery of a dead body in the den: shock, denial, horror. 'And Daddy is Christopher's daddy, too?' he gasped. When I confirmed this, he began to cry—wet, sad sobbing."

The Unexpected Letdown

When Andrea was pregnant with her second child, she made a point of preparing four-year-old Carolyn for the arrival of her new brother. In the evenings, they would snuggle together on the couch, talking and reading stories about babies. Andrea took Carolyn to sibling classes at the hospital. As the date approached, she let Carolyn help prepare the baby's room and bought her a little baby boy doll. She regularly assured her daughter that she loved her very much and always would.

Carolyn responded warmly to this attention. She often patted Andrea's protruding tummy and laughed when she felt movement. She would press her face close and chat with her baby brother. "I was thrilled and relieved that Carolyn was so excited," Andrea recalled. "Her happiness just made me glow."

But this idyllic environment changed the moment John came home from the hospital. "None of us were prepared for the extra strain of having a new baby around the house," Andrea admitted. "I was tired a lot in those early days. I wanted to rest more, and Carolyn was often angry at me because I was feeling less energetic and playful. Before John was born, she basked in my exclusive attention. Planning for the baby was lots of fun; actually having him in the house was not much fun. I was busy with John—babies require a lot of care!—and Carolyn felt shortchanged."

Andrea was disappointed that Carolyn wasn't more enthusiastic once John arrived. Although she was often angry at her mom, Carolyn seemed only mildly interested in her brother. When her preschool teacher asked about the baby, Carolyn was dismissive. "Oh . . . *him!* He sleeps or cries or poops all the time."

It was Andrea's hope that Carolyn would become more responsive as John grew older. But instead, she went from being indifferent to being increasingly annoyed with her brother. "When John started to toddle around, things really became hard. Carolyn was extremely resentful whenever he disturbed her. And, of course, he was attracted to her like a magnet. I'll never forget one afternoon after she had spent hours setting up her Fisher Price zoo. John came lurching along and crashed right into it—with an oblivious grin. Carolyn was so upset she almost bit him. She stopped herself in time because I happened to walk into the room. I think she knew how furious I'd be if she did bite her brother."

Meanwhile, Carolyn was becoming moody and argumentative at home and at school. Andrea observed, "It seemed like the only two people in the world who mattered to her were her father and me, and she was distraught about losing a big chunk of our attention to John. She saw that we adored her baby brother, who was uncomplicated, cheerful and carefree—all the things she wasn't at that moment."

Andrea's experience and her insight brought home just how difficult the introduction of a sibling can be—even in the most loving home, and in spite of the best-laid plans. There's simply no way to prepare for all the inevitabilities. Andrea's experience was one I would hear repeatedly, in different variations, as I talked with parents who had taken the leap from one child to two, or more than two.

Of course, the adjustment is different depending on the age of your first child. In *The Emotional Life of the Toddler*, Alicia Lieberman paints a vivid picture of the practical ways a toddler experiences the difference: "He now needs to wait more often and longer than ever before for things he wants or needs. He spends more time alone. He is scolded or corrected more frequently as parents try to teach him what he can and cannot do with the baby. Some favorite activities—going swimming, going to the playground, playing a favorite game—often have to be curtailed or postponed because of the baby's needs. Things cannot be done spontaneously any more because the baby's schedule needs to be taken into account, and the time it takes to prepare the baby's bag can seem interminable. These are important losses for a toddler." As a rule, it tends to be easier for children to make the adjustment to a new sibling when they are a little older, and when the age gap is greater. But don't assume that rule is hard and fast. As most parents have learned the hard way, all rules are made to be broken.

When Number One Protests

Parents aren't always prepared for the reactions of their firstborns. They may expect their children to share their warm and happy feelings, but they are unsure how to handle the brutally honest responses of their older children to the new baby. One mother wryly related the following conversation with her three-year-old, Mark:

MOM:　You're so good to your baby brother. Isn't he cute?
MARK:　Yeah, he's okay, but maybe we could move his crib down to the basement with the kitty's litter box.

Another mom got this response when she told her seven-year-old about her pregnancy:

MOM: Guess what! We're going to have a baby. You're going to have a little brother or sister. What do you think of that?

TERI: (vehemently) I hate babies! They stink, and all they do is make doody in their pants.

At times, children's resentful feelings can be disguised as excessive, smothering love. A horrified mother happened upon her four-year-old daughter cheerfully burying the two-month-old in pillows. "My God! What are you doing?" she screeched, pushing her daughter away and grabbing the pillows. "You'll kill him." Her daughter began to sob loudly, crushed by the force of her mother's accusation. "He couldn't sleep. I was only making him quiet and cozy," she finally gasped through her tears.

No matter how carefully you break the news, it's going to take a small child a while to digest it. Don't expect your child's initial reaction to the news to be the end of the matter. Children are masters of imagination; they can weave unexpected scenarios once they've had a chance to think things over. Yvonne described how Elena, her four-year-old, surprised her this way. "We told her about my pregnancy fairly early on, at about four months," Yvonne said. "She seemed okay about it, but one day she came home from school kind of mopey. I held her in my lap and we had this conversation.

YVONNE: What's on your mind, honey?

ELENA: Nothing . . .

YVONNE: You seem sad.

ELENA: (burrowing her face into Yvonne's lap) Because I have to find a new family.

YVONNE: Oh?

ELENA: Because you are getting married again and having another baby.

"I was caught completely off guard by her statement," Yvonne admitted. "She was having all of these fantasies about the new baby, and I never realized it. In her mind, you get married and you have a child. One marriage, one child. She thought if I was going to have another baby, it must mean I was getting married again, and she would have to go live somewhere else. I reassured her, and her father reassured her, but we were amazed by her misconceptions. I think I really understood how vulnerable a child can feel. All these big adults are making decisions without you and you have no control."

Jealousy Is Normal

Even when the transition appears to go smoothly, when you've prepped your firstborn in every way for the event, that doesn't mean everything is completely resolved in the eldest child's mind. Kids have surprising ways of interpreting information. So, even though you may think you've explained everything, and your child seems to understand, you might discover differently. One mother told me this story: "At first, my son was very excited when he found out he was going to have a baby brother or sister. I took him to visit my friends who had recently given birth, and he seemed fascinated by their babies. When his brother was born, I let him help pick a name and choose baby toys. I told him that I would always love him no matter what. He seemed quite content. But as his brother got older, he became troubled. One day he asked me out of the blue, 'Why did you have to have him? Wasn't I good enough?' "

Another parent, Anna, looked back with humor on the introduction of baby Nicky to three-year-old Angela. "The initial meeting was so beautiful," Anna said. "When Angela first saw Nicky she was full of wonder and amazement at someone smaller than her. It was such a picture-perfect moment that we got out the camera and took a photo. We decided to use it for our Christmas card—our two children looking so loving toward each other. But," she said, laughing, "by the time Christmas rolled around three months later, the bloom was off the rose. Angela's face was in a permanent scowl. She couldn't stand her little brother. My husband and I said, 'Boy, it's a good thing we took our Christmas card picture three months ago!' "

As adults, we can feel some compassion for the only child who is suddenly faced with having to share his or her parents' love and attention with a sibling. A mother who complained because her eldest daughter always horned in when she was reading to the youngest realized in a moment of insight, "My youngest doesn't mind sharing, probably because she's never had the experience of being the 'only.' I can see why my older daughter would miss that, but I began to understand why the second child doesn't feel deprived. She had never had me all to herself so she didn't miss it."

Another mother noticed how much her second child enjoyed it when the third was born. "It was an entirely different experience," she marveled. "Jody wasn't at all jealous of her baby brother, the way Spence was with her. She was delighted. I think since she was never an 'only,' she had more tolerance for a new addition."

Getting Ready for Number Two

Every piece of advice about preparing your first child for the arrival of a sibling must be offered with a caveat: There's no foolproof method. That's because your child, as you have discovered, is a complex and unpredictable individual who has a mind of his or her own. Sometimes parents do all the recommended things to prepare for the new arrival, only to find that their efforts seem to have been in vain. Other parents do little or nothing at all, and the relationship works out quite smoothly.

Although no methods are one hundred percent effective, many parents have shared creative ideas for making the adjustment. I'd like to pass along some of my favorites.

Breaking the News . . .

- Wait to tell your child (particularly a toddler or preschooler) until three or four months before the birth, if you can. Nine or even seven months is too long a time for a young child to anticipate.

- On the other hand, don't wait too long. Your child should hear the news from you, not from someone else.
- Encourage questions: "How did that baby get in your stomach?" "How does a baby get out?" Answer them in an age-appropriate way. Let children know the correct words for body parts: penis, not "pee-pee"; uterus, not "tummy"; vagina, not "down there."
- Don't tell a child how he will feel—"You're going to love having a baby sister!"

Before the Baby Comes . . .

- Take your first child along on doctor's visits.
- Sign your child up for sibling preparation classes, if you can. They're often offered free at the hospital. Be sure the class is age appropriate.
- Ask your child to help you pick out a name for the baby.
- Visit a friend who has had a new baby.
- Let your child feel the baby kicking.
- Talk about what it will be like when the baby comes, stressing the positives of being a big brother or a big sister, and all the things an older kid can do that a baby can't.
- Don't paint too rosy a picture of what a new baby is like. Help the older child realize that a baby takes a long time before he can become a playmate.
- Role-play "Mom goes to the hospital and comes home with a baby," using dolls.
- Show your child his own baby pictures and reminisce fondly about when he was a baby. Also, use it as an opportunity to remind him how much he has learned to do and how competent he is: "Look at this picture. It's the first time you stood up all by yourself. And now look at you. You're racing all over the place."

- Let your child pick out a toy for the baby.
- Let your child participate in decorating and preparing the baby's space. Set up the playpen, swing, changing table, or whatever new item you're buying in advance so your child can get used to seeing them.
- If they will have separate rooms, make a ritual of moving your child from the "old" baby's room to the "new" big kid's room well before the arrival of the baby.
- Read books about a new baby coming. There are wonderful resources available at your local bookstore or library.
- Show your child the hospital or maternity center where the baby will be born. Many hospitals have tours for siblings, and it will help comfort your child to know where Mommy is going when she disappears to have the baby.

When Mommy's in the Hospital . . .

- Before you go to the hospital, tape-record your child's favorite bedtime stories so he can hear your voice at bedtime.
- Take a wrapped toy, such as a large stuffed animal, to the hospital and present it to your eldest child if she visits you after the birth. Or prepare a couple of small gifts or notes to be given to your child while you're away from home.
- Tape a picture of your first child to the inside of the baby's bassinet—where Number One can see it.
- Let your child hold the baby as soon as possible, while sitting on the floor to prevent dropping.
- When you call your child on the phone from the hospital, make sure to talk about his activities or concerns, resisting the urge to prattle on about the cute new baby.

After the Baby Comes Home . . .

- When you get home, make it your first priority to give the oldest child a big hug while someone else holds the baby.

- Let your child help with small tasks where appropriate—feeding, changing, fetching, rocking, washing, holding—with careful supervision, of course. And don't forget to thank or praise him for being helpful.
- Divide your time so one parent pays special attention to the oldest child while the other is caring for the baby. If you're a single parent, plan special time with your eldest when the baby is sleeping, or swap time with a friend or neighbor.
- Ask your child if she'd like to draw pictures for the baby that you can put near the crib.
- Make an effort to praise your older child's accomplishments, like going to the toilet on her own. At the same time, expect and allow for some babyish behavior and regression, such as baby talk, bottles, accidents, and so on.
- Try to maintain a routine that is as close to the old one as possible. Be particularly sensitive to maintaining favorite rituals—like bedtime stories or games.
- Tell your baby in the older child's presence how lucky she is to have a big brother or sister who can make her laugh, get her things, play games with her, or rock her gently.
- Don't give the baby special items that belonged to your first child—like a favorite blanket or rattle—without first asking permission. Allow your child to choose which toys or "snugglies" he may want to pass on to the baby.
- If your child wants to be a baby again, let him "play" at being baby. (He'll get tired of the game as soon as he remembers how little a baby can do!)
- Ask your child to translate what he thinks the baby wants. Then praise him: "You seem to understand the baby better than anyone."

How to Handle the Tough Issues

The tips detailed in the previous pages will give you some suggestions for easing the transition. But what do you do when things do go wrong? While many families manage to roll with the punches and get through the introduction of a new sibling with relative calm, many other parents are baffled by disruptions they're not sure how to handle. Here are some of the most common:

🕭 *Number one wants to be baby.*

It helps to be sensitive to the eldest child's need to sometimes be the baby. Miriam experienced this with her eighteen-month-old:

"Sam wasn't too thrilled to have a new baby in the house, but he wasn't actively hostile toward her," Miriam said. "He wanted to nurse again when he saw me nursing her, but much to my relief he found it very unpalatable. Before Lisa was born, I had let Sam feel the baby kicking, and on the night I went to the hospital, I gave him his own doll so we'd both have a baby. He never really played with it, though. The one aspect of my relationship with Sam which was difficult around the time of Lisa's birth was toilet training. With hindsight, I think I pushed too hard at the wrong time, and I was totally lacking in patience. Looking back, I can now see how much Sam was still clinging to being a baby, and his lack of cooperation over toilet training was a natural outcome of his feelings and fears. I wish I had handled matters differently and lowered my expectations. But the idea of having two in diapers was so frustrating."

Regression is very common and is to be expected. After all, the baby's getting lots of attention and pampering. When he cries, he gets picked up and comforted. When he's hungry, everyone rushes to feed him. The older child may be thinking, "What's so great about being big and having to do things for myself?"

Pat described how she handled Penny, six, when she wanted to be babied. "After her sister was born, Penny started asking me to dress her every morning. I gave in because I felt she needed the extra attention. But it got to the point where I couldn't get her off to school unless I dressed her. I was getting annoyed, and a bit concerned, too. I considered stopping 'cold turkey'—no more getting dressed by Mommy—but that seemed harsh. I tried to find some kind of compromise that we could both live with, and came up with the following solution."

PAT: I think sometimes you like to be treated like a baby.

PENNY: Uh-huh . . .

PAT: It's fun to have Mommy dress you and pretend you're little.

PENNY: I like it when you dress me. I want you to.

PAT: I have an idea. Let's choose one day every week and call it Baby Day. I'll dress you and cuddle you and you can pretend you're a baby. And the other days you can be a big girl and dress yourself. What do you think?

PENNY: Okay. Tuesdays will be my Baby Day.

"I turned it into a game, and we had a lot of fun with it," Pat said. "Penny started dressing herself on the other days, and it worked great. Eventually, she grew impatient with Baby Day and started dressing herself on Tuesdays, too."

❧ Number one feels left out.

In her book, *Child-Wise,* Cathy Tempelsman relates one mother's creative idea for helping her eldest feel special after the baby came:

"If Brandon and I were reading a book together and the baby started to cry, I never rushed over to her. I would say to him, 'What are we going to do?' It was always Brandon's idea to go over and see what was the matter. After a few months, he was the one who got the biggest smiles from Stephanie, so we called him the baby expert. You could see that he loved that. Instead of the baby making him less important in the house, she made him more important."

Beverly, a mother from my group, made a special point of mentioning four-year-old Cheryl's competence, compared to the baby's. For example, one day when the baby was crying because he was hungry, Beverly sighed with exaggerated annoyance.

BEVERLY: Boy, that baby can sure be a pain!

CHERYL: (enthusiastically joining in) Yeah, he cries too much. He's always hungry.

BEVERLY: I can't wait till he gets big enough to get his own juice from the refrigerator—like you can. And learn to pour it without spilling, too.

CHERYL: Yeah, I can do it all by myself. I don't have to cry all the time.

BEVERLY: (rolling her eyes) Oh, well, you know babies! What can you do?

CHERYL: (mimicking her mother's tone of voice) Yeah, what can you do?

"I felt a little guilty about saying that," Beverly said. "But I figured he didn't know it, so it didn't hurt him. And it made Cheryl feel a sense of pride. We were allies."

See if you can find occasions to deliberately put the baby's needs on hold while you attend to the older child's needs. For example, you might say, "Wait, baby, I can't get you your bottle just this second. Johnny needs his juice now." It won't hurt the baby to wait a couple of minutes, and your older child will see that his needs are not always going to come last now that there's a baby in the house.

Debbie made a special effort to let her older daughter Emma know how much she appreciated her competence. "For example," she said, "sometimes when Scott was playing in his crib, I would hold Emma and say to Scott, 'Emma and I are going to color now. You can't color yet because you are still a baby. This is just for big kids.' And we go color. Emma always gets a big smile and proudly announces, 'No babies. Emma big kid.' It makes her feel special, and it gives us one-on-one time."

🍃 *Number one expresses negative feelings.*

As uncomfortable as it might be to hear your children express anger, jealousy, or resentment, try to remember that thinking and feeling are very different from doing. These emotions are perfectly natural and need to be aired. If you can acknowledge and "hear" your child when she expresses negative feelings toward the baby, she will feel as though you understand her.

When a parent can listen with empathy to her child's anger, the child doesn't feel like a "bad" person for feeling what he feels—as Mike's mom related. "I had been playing with six-month-old Michelle, when four-year-old Mike grabbed a toy from her and threw it across the room."

MOM: Are you angry about something?

MIKE: *Yes!!*

MOM: What's making you angry?

MIKE: I'm angry at you.

MOM: Why?

MIKE: I don't know. I just am.

MOM: Do you sometimes wish Michelle wasn't here?

MIKE: Yes. Take her back to the hospital.

MOM: Sometimes you would like all of my attention all the time.

MIKE: Yes. I don't love you. I love my daddy, not you.

MOM: Well, I love you.

MIKE: Well, don't love me.

MOM: I always love you, even when I get angry at you. You know, you can still love somebody and be angry at them.

MIKE: People make me angry. When they scream at me I get mad.

MOM: So, when I scream, it makes you angry?

MIKE: Yes!

MOM: I'll tell you what. I'll try not to scream so much. But you need to remember not to hit. Can you do that?

MIKE: Okay, Mommy.

"Later, when I was changing Michelle's diaper, Mike began hitting me on my thigh. Ordinarily, I'd scream, 'Will you stop that!' but this time I said, 'You said you'd try not to hit.' He stopped and was terrific the rest of the night—angelic, in fact."

Expect to have moments when your older child expresses negative feelings about the new baby. In *Raising Brothers and Sisters without Raising the Roof*, Carole and Andrew Calladine offer an example. They write, "Another child, hearing her parents discuss the possible sex of the next child, listened in growing agitation:

MOM: I hope it's a boy.
DAD: I would like a girl.
CHILD: I hope it isn't anything."

Sharon, a woman who recently gave birth to her second child, a daughter, shared this dialogue she had with her three-year-old son, Josh, a few weeks before the baby was born, in which he clearly expressed his ambivalent feelings to his mom.

JOSH: Where will the baby live when it gets born?
MOM: The baby will live here in our house.
JOSH: (seeming shocked) Here? In *our* house?
MOM: Yes, remember you helped me fix up the room.
JOSH: Maybe we can give the baby to someone who doesn't have one.
MOM: The baby would be sad not to have a smart, wonderful big brother like you.
JOSH: Yeah. I'm going to go draw a picture for the baby's room.

Jeri supplied this dialogue showing how she dealt with four-year-old Susie's reaction to her baby sister. "Susie was thrilled and proud to be a big sister, and we always did our best to make her feel loved and needed. But when Emily began to crawl and get into Susie's things, her attitude changed. She complained to me one day:

SUSIE: I don't want a baby sister anymore.

JERI: Why not?

SUSIE: She ruins everything. She gets in all my stuff.

JERI: I remember when I was your age, I felt the same way about Uncle Jack.

SUSIE: Uncle Jack was a baby?

JERI: Yes, and I always had to put my toys away so he wouldn't get into them. Being a big sister isn't easy.

SUSIE: Yeah!

Reflecting on the conversation, Jeri said, "I was about to give her my 'You shouldn't feel that way, she's your sister' lecture, but I stopped myself. Instead, I listened to her and tried to acknowledge her feelings and tell her about my own experience. She was fascinated, and now she often asks about when Uncle Jack was a baby. It's something we share." Another parent suggested having the child make a book about the baby, listing the things that are fun and the things that are not fun:

Fun	*Not Fun*
He laughs when I smooch him on his tummy.	He cries, cries, cries.
	He smells like doody.
He tries to kick me when I go near his crib.	He always wants to be carried.
He likes to suck on my finger.	

Let your child know that it's safe to express his or her anger toward the new baby, as long as there's no hurting. To some extent, anger and jealousy are inevitable, yet must be directed away from the baby. One parent established an Angry Corner for her daughter Syl. Whenever the baby got on Syl's nerves or messed with her toys and made her mad, Syl went to the Angry Corner. There, she had permission to say, "I hate the baby, I hate the baby" or draw pictures of her "ugly" little brother or punch her punching bag. Once she had finished venting, Syl often returned to play with her brother.

This, Too, Shall Pass

Maybe the most helpful thing of all is the realization that the adjustment period is finite. It doesn't last forever—even though it may seem that way at the time. Sibling relationships are always in a state of flux. Sometimes, when you least expect it, your kids will surprise you by showing a different side to their feelings.

Peggy told my workshop group how worried she was about how much her six-year-old son, Arthur, seemed to despise his baby sister. "He's never been happy with her, but now that the baby is vertical, Arthur considers her a real annoyance," Peggy said. "He especially can't bear how much everyone, especially my husband, responds to her charm and cuteness. I caught a glimpse of Arthur's face when he noticed his dad was adoring the baby and saw a look of pure misery. He's become more argumentative with me, too." She complained, "I hardly recognize him. Everything is a battle. He used to be such an outgoing, upbeat child."

Paula, another parent in the group, commented, "Arthur sounds very needy right now. What if you could spend some time alone with him and say something like, 'I really miss being alone with you. Would you like to go walking through the woods with me tomorrow? Maybe we can look for mushrooms together. The baby can't go because she's too young.'"

A couple of weeks later, Peggy appeared in the group with a changed attitude. This, she explained brightly, was due to the fact that she and Arthur had been able to travel alone to the city together the previous weekend. "He was delightful company," she said. "He seemed to blossom having me all to himself. We had a wonderful time." Peggy was also astonished by the way Arthur had responded when she told him that the baby couldn't go. "He seemed very sad and disappointed. He said, 'Oh, why can't she go, too?'" In this way, Peggy began to discover that the developing sibling relationship isn't so cut and dried, after all. She noticed from Arthur's response that in addition to being jealous and resentful, he also has many loving and protective feelings toward his sister. It made her day.

Chapter 3

The Toughest Job in the World

"I identify with that scene in the movie *Ben-Hur*," a mother of two told me ruefully. "It's like my life is the chariot race, and I'm the one who has fallen off the chariot and is being dragged and trampled."

Her experience is more common than she realizes. Since 80 percent of all mothers work outside the home, at least part-time, and 52 percent of them have children under one year old, being a parent of more than one has become more stressful than ever. The sheer uphill battle of surviving each day—getting the kids up, dressed, fed, and off to school, racing to work, hurrying home to messy houses and piles of laundry and dinner to be cooked—can demoralize parents. There's never a break. If it sounds depressing and unremittingly negative, that's the way many parents experience it. I try to find ways to help ease the stress, to encourage them to lighten up and not be so hard on themselves. I remember well how tired I myself felt at the end of a day with my demanding young sons. How my eyelids would flicker and I'd doze off as soon as I sat down; how I'd slump against the edge of the tub while they were taking their baths; how I constantly watched the hands of the clock crawl toward eight—bedtime; how I'd try to keep my voice animated and cheerful and my attention focused on them when what I really wanted was to get them in bed, turn off the light, close the door, and be done for the day. It's not an admission I'm particularly proud of, but fatigue can do that to you.

Most people would agree that being a parent should be defined by the joys and pleasures of having children, not by the strains of making physical, emotional, and often financial ends meet. One of the most frequent questions parents ask is "How can I balance everything I need to do?" It's a topic we discuss often in my workshop groups. In fact, it sometimes seems to be the most consistent theme of all—the sense that there's just too much to do and not enough time in which to do it. As one parent so eloquently put it, "My ability to be a good parent is in direct proportion to how much sleep I got the night before."

"I Used to Be in Control!"

I am convinced that one of the biggest reasons we parents get so frustrated with the upheaval that accompanies kids is that we can't adjust to not being in control. Many of the parents I meet are very bright people, accustomed to doing well at their jobs. They're good managers, adept at problem solving. They come to parenting with loads of self-assurance, competence, and organizational skills. But they soon discover that the skills that served them so well in their careers are rarely transferable to child raising.

Recently, Jenny, the mother of three young children, came to me for advice because she couldn't get out from under. "The crazy thing is," she said, "I used to be such a control freak. I prided myself on being Miss Efficiency. But when I try to apply those skills to managing my kids, it doesn't fly."

Like many of today's mothers who have achieved success in the workplace, Jenny was frustrated because the skills she had mastered didn't work with her kids. But why would they? One reason you can't apply the same skills to child raising is because your kids don't share your goals. When you need to get out the door and to your office or her school, your child is suddenly transfixed by the dog scratching fleas. You can't "manage" him. Parents who view their children as "part of a team" are in for a rude awakening when they try to reach a consensus on anything at all. We need a different set of skills and expectations for this job!

Today's parents often experience an intensified pressure to measure up to even greater standards than they set for themselves. That's especially true for families that don't fit the old "nuclear" family mode—single-parent families, families with stepchildren, families with gay and lesbian parents, and other nonconventional arrangements. But as someone accurately observed, "Donna Reed and June Cleaver were perfect mommies because they only had to do it thirty minutes a week."

All Work and No Play

The majority of parents I hear from confirm the fact that today's families are stressed to the max.

"I did not anticipate how difficult a second child would be," Sheryl said. She had looked forward joyfully to the birth of her daughter. "Being an only child, I had no idea of the volcanic upheaval of feelings and the sheer exhaustion which would come from having two children instead of one. One thing that *has* helped is that in the last year I hired more sitters. My single biggest expense after rent is child care. I also have support from my friends who have small children. But still, I often feel overwhelmed and very, very tired."

When both parents work full-time outside the home, the pressures can be dizzying. Barbara, a working mother of two, complained that she couldn't seem to get her life organized. She sighed, "Our house is always a wreck. You might think, no big deal, but I need neatness and order. Before we had kids, our house was sparkling. Now it's a losing battle just to keep it minimally respectable."

"You sound discouraged," I commiserated.

"I hate living this way," Barbara said passionately. "I am very often at a fever pitch of frustration, and go ranting and raving all over the house, desperately and futilely straightening up. Sometimes I feel like two different people. At work, I'm the cool, competent professional, utterly unflappable. At home, I'm like a maniac."

Denise, the mother of two sons, who worked full-time for a large law firm, freely admitted to my workshop group that one of the reasons she loved going to her job every day was that she was treated with respect. "At work, I'm seen as an adult," she said. "They call me Mrs. B. I like that. Nobody ever whines at me. The people I supervise never say, 'It's not fair! June got an easier assignment.' And the best part of all is that my work is really appreciated. People say, 'Nice job,' or 'Thanks for your help.' At home, nobody pats you on the back."

The others in the group found the very idea of such praise hilarious. "Can't you just imagine?" Jennifer laughed, mimicking a child: " 'Thank you, Mommy dearest, for preparing such a lovely dinner. It's so nice that you take care of me and make sure my teeth are brushed so I won't have cavities. You're doing such a good job raising me.' "

Everyone enjoyed the moment of humor—and they also got the point. As one woman put it, "Being a parent means waiting a long time for appreciation. Kids are by nature self-involved, so they can't help taking us for granted."

Bonnie's experience was similar to Denise's. "Work is a refuge in many respects, because it takes me away from home and recharges me," she said. "When both my children were very young there was a time when I couldn't wait to go on a business trip. The idea of staying in a hotel and not having to make a bed or a meal or be wakened three times during the night—it was pure heaven!"

Hearing these mothers talk, I also realized that the oversimplification that working mothers had more stress than mothers who stayed home didn't necessarily hold true either. Although the lives of working moms are certainly hectic, they have advantages that aren't available to mothers who are at home full-time.

Full-time Moms Have Their Own Stresses

I hear mothers with outside jobs turning wistful as they imagine what it would be like if they were home. Often, they say something like, "Oh, wouldn't it be wonderful not to have to rush to work every morning!" They assume that mothers who don't work outside the home have all this glorious extra time. But the reality is quite different. I have found that women who are home full-time have their own set of daily stresses that can be every bit as frustrating.

The truth is that women who work at home don't necessarily have the best of both worlds. "I'm constantly being interrupted," complained Elaine, a freelance designer. "I'm the one who gets asked to be a class mother, or who fills in when the babysitter doesn't show up, or who is expected to drop everything to shuttle the kids to their after-school activities. And when my husband gets home, I'd like him to take up the slack. But he's tired from work and naturally doesn't feel like it. He figures that since I've been home all day with the kids and he's been out working, my time is less valuable."

And Susan, a self-employed writer and mother of two, said, "Being self-employed and working at home can be even more stressful than going to an office every day. I can't walk away from it. I get phone calls at all hours of the day and evening. And it's very hard to say to a client, 'I can't deal with this right now. Benny is about to scratch his sister's eyes out.' "

"I learned that when you supposedly 'don't work,' you can be overwhelmed by volunteer activities—Girl Scouts, Sunday school, class mother, bake sales, et cetera," said Linda. "All it really means is that you work without getting paid. Now that I'm back at my job, I have the freedom to say no to these demands with less guilt."

Frequently mothers who stay home report that they get little respect. "If my husband walks in the door after work and sees me drooping, he just can't understand it," said the mother of three children under age eight. He'll say, 'How come you're always so tired? You're not working.' Which, of course, infuriates me. And sometimes after dinner when I'm trying to get three kids bathed and into bed, I'll go looking for help and find him in the living room calmly reading the paper with classical music playing, and I'll want to scream, 'You've got to be kidding!' "

One of my parents revealed what is unfortunately a common experience for these mothers who are not working for pay. She said: "When I introduce myself as an at-home parent, people drift away, assuming I'm either stupid or boring."

Too often, stay-at-home mothers introduce themselves apologetically: "I'm just a mother," or "No, I don't work." It makes me angry and sad to hear it. If only they could eliminate that denigrating word *just*. I admire one of the mothers in my workshops who defines her role by saying, "I'm a household administrator."

Full-time moms are often in a position of having to defend their choice not to work outside the home. It's a sad reflection on our society's values when a mother has to feel guilty about doing something as important as raising another human being!

Stop Comparing Yourself to Others

Many parents just can't resist comparing themselves and their children with others who seem in their eyes to be doing it so much better. As a mother in my workshop lamented recently, "We went to a wedding and it was *my* kids who were running up and down the aisle, *my* kids who were giggling during the ceremony, *my* kids who spilled punch on the dance floor at the reception. Everyone else's kids were perfectly behaved." I could sympathize with this mother's chagrin, because at those times it seems like everyone is staring at you and judging you. You can't help thinking, "What's the matter with my kids?" And, of course, the extension of that is "What's the matter with *me*?"

Franny experienced a "reality check" just when she was starting to feel discouraged. "My oldest son was so difficult, and I had a very close friend whose son was a piece of cake," she recalled. "I always thought she must be a much better mother than me, and she was too polite to say anything when she saw my son having a total meltdown while hers sat quietly coloring. And then she gave birth to a daughter who was very tough to handle, and she actually admitted to me, 'You know, I have to tell you, I used to compare myself to you, thinking how much better a parent I was when you couldn't control your child. Now, I finally see that it wasn't you and it wasn't me. It was them!' "

Fathers Are Essential

There's an important new movement under way promoting the idea of men becoming more involved in their children's lives. In practice, though, many mothers complain that their spouses do not contribute equally on the parenting front. For one thing, many men are simply not *there* to contribute. Other men just don't see how absolutely essential their role is.

Marilyn's complaint is one I hear often. She and her husband have two children, a boy and a girl, both in elementary school. Both parents work outside the home. Yet, said Marilyn, "I do ninety percent of the child care. My husband is a devoted father, but he sees his role as having fun with the kids, not doing chores that are related to their care. I often feel resentful and I rarely take time for myself. My personal time is usually my time in the office. I almost never see my friends, read, or exercise."

"My husband works long hours and sometimes on the weekends," Celia, the mother of two, told me. "Although I have a part-time career as a management consultant and also do volunteer work, I'm responsible for the child rearing. My husband 'pitches in,' but he is more of a baby-sitter than a parent. He doesn't value my work. For instance, he's agreed to give me a day off on Saturday, but he usually finds a way to whittle it down to half a day."

When I suggested to Celia that she explain to her husband how she felt and see if she could solicit more of his cooperation, she laughed sarcastically. "Oh, I already tried that! He made a big production of doing more with the kids, but in his care my son has been bitten by a dog, fallen down and lost a tooth, and had his favorite teddy bear stolen right out of his stroller at the park. I have a name for this phenomenon.

I call it 'The Tyranny of Incompetence.' I think my husband knows that if he does a lousy job, I'll take back all of the duties."

"And does it work?" I asked.

"I'm afraid so," Celia sighed. "What choice do I have? Wait until they start losing limbs?"

Vera, the mother of two girls, runs a business from her home. Although she works very hard, she feels that because she's at home, she gets saddled with almost all of the responsibility for managing the house and children. "Anything my husband does is seen as 'helping' me," she said. "It's always like he's doing me a favor, and then he expects to be praised for days on end. I have not been able to get him to willingly take responsibility for the kids for years—and I have tried and tried. Before, when we had only one child, I didn't mind so much, but now I really need him and he's not there. I've pretty much given up."

This is a legitimate complaint. But sometimes we mothers don't recognize our own complicity in the status quo. For example, a frequent theme that comes up in my workshops is what I call the Let-Get Syndrome: "How do I *get* my husband to . . . ?" or "Should I *let* my husband . . . ?" Women want and need their spouses to help out more, but they don't always see how they sabotage men's efforts to be equal partners by insisting that everything be done on *their* own terms. One mother, in laughing acknowledgment of this tendency, recalled how she was so exhausted at the end of one day that she yelled at her husband, "I've had it! You take over." She stormed upstairs, but was back in five minutes, asking why their daughter wasn't in her pajamas yet, and expressing disapproval at the TV program they were watching. She admitted, "I told him to take over, but I really meant, 'Take over, but do it the way *I* do it.' "

When Theresa, the mother of four children under age ten, started a part-time job working every other weekend, she found that the changes in routine ended up being positive. "This has become one of the best things for my husband," she said. "He has had to take care of the kids and he manages very well. He can handle sports events, ice skating, birthday parties, and diapers like a pro. I'm sure he wouldn't have learned to cope as well if I was always home. Of course, I've made allowances. I've had to accept that the way the kids are dressed or the amount of time they nap or what they eat for snacks are not my ways. But those things aren't nearly as important as my husband's confidence as a dad and his increasing closeness with the children."

Overly stressed mothers may have a tendency to see their husbands as the "bad guys" when they are seen as not offering enough support. But sometimes these moms don't realize how much fathers are made to feel superfluous. Sally was faced with a surprising and painful revelation when her husband Joe let her know exactly how he felt. "I was always nagging him to help out more," Sally said. "The minute he walked in from work, I was on his case. The truth is, I was growing quite fond of my self-righteousness." Sally shared this dialogue of a moment of truth.

SALLY: Why do I always have to beg for your help?

JOE: (growing angry) Look, I do my best. For your information, I work very hard at being a part of this family, and I get rejected at every turn.

SALLY: (defensively) What do you mean? How can you say that?

JOE: You and the kids have your own little thing going, and I come home and am treated like an extra. You give orders, the kids go, 'I want Mommy to bathe me,' or 'I want Mommy to read me a story.'

SALLY: I don't mean to shut you out.

JOE: Maybe not. But you manage to sabotage me when I do try to have some fun with the kids. Like the other night, I know I came home late and you wanted to get the kids to bed, but was it so important that you had to interrupt our wrestling session?

SALLY: You disrupted the routine. I was just getting them settled down.

"At that point," Sally said later, "a light flashed in my head. Suddenly, I really heard what Joe was saying, and I realized it was true. I *was* shutting him out. I was running my own little family and getting resentful when he tried to be a part of it in his own particular way. It was a very hard thing to hear. But after that, we were able to talk more frankly for the first time about how we both felt—me overburdened and Joe rejected. We decided that it didn't have to be that way, and we made some changes. For instance, Joe planned a special time with each child during the week where they went out together or played board games. I saw how the kids responded to his attention and realized they hadn't really appreciated him. In the end, I was grateful that Joe confronted me."

Fathers rarely have good role models for how to be equal partners in parenting. The majority of fathers I've met were raised in families where all the action revolved around Mom. As one man related, "Dad was the guy who walked in the door at six o'clock, delivered spankings for the transgressions that Mom reported, and spent the evening dozing in front of the TV. On Saturdays, he mowed the lawn and fixed the car. He was my idol, but he didn't teach me very much about being the kind of father I want to be to my children." Other fathers give similar accounts.

And one theme that comes up a lot is that the previous generation of fathers spent virtually no time with their daughters. Gerald, the father of two girls, remembered, "In my family, the boys 'belonged' to Dad and the girls 'belonged' to Mom. Girl stuff was completely outside my dad's realm. He was visibly uncomfortable whenever he had to deal with girl problems. I certainly don't feel the same way. I want to be involved with my daughters. But I have to find my own way."

Eleven Ways to Relieve Your Stress

The following tips may be helpful in diminishing some of the demands that can wear us down.

❧ *1. Start by saying, "Not guilty!"*

Guilt is the number one barrier to effective parenting. As the author Vicki Lansky put it so well, "Parenting and guilt go together like peanut butter and jelly." It's a given. And too much advice for parents merely reinforces their guilt instead of liberating them. So, I suggest that we start by saying, "Not guilty!"

With all the pressure we put on ourselves, no wonder we often feel so crummy when we face the everyday stresses of our lives. Here are some of the shamefaced "realities" I managed to pull out of my workshop parents. I'm sure you can add your own. We all could:

"I rush them every morning and end up yelling."

"In the evenings I'm often so tired I try to skip pages when I'm reading a story—and they catch me every time."

"Cooking is such a pain. I end up taking them to Burger King."

"I skip baths and let them stay up past their bedtime because sometimes it seems it's just too much hassle."

"The cookies I send on snack day are never homemade."

"I don't get home from work until six o'clock."

"I missed my son's first soccer game."

"I lose my temper and am an incessant nag."

"I make the twins nap for at least an hour a day, whether they need to or not."

"I hate to play games and almost never do."

"I didn't take time to check my daughter's homework and she got an F."

"I broke the rule and let my son stay in our bed because I just didn't have the energy to get up and walk him back to his room."

"So, how do you feel about this list?" I asked when we were finished.

"We are very, very bad mothers and we'll never get an A in parenting!" one woman replied with mock sobriety, and we all laughed, with a sense of relief at the rare chance to lighten up.

We'll be talking about guilt a lot in this book. To me, guilt is like the big boulder in the road. It gets in the way of everything else. You cannot feel confident and assured if you feel guilty. And by the same token, you can't help your children develop self-esteem if they look at you and see a person who is apologizing all over the place for being human. I hope that as you read this book, you will find new solutions for your own circumstances from the accumulated wisdom of other parents. And when you see that you're not the only parent who is full of imperfections, I hope this realization will help you to be much less hard on yourself. Remember, it's only the caring parents who struggle!

I try to remind parents that the first step is to reconnect with what is possible and acknowledge that since they can't do it all, maybe they can allow themselves to not even try.

One of my favorite tips comes from Ann Pleshette Murphy, editor in chief of *Parents* magazine. As a full-time working mom, Annie has adopted the policy "Don't add unless you can subtract." If you're making cookies for the school bake sale, let the laundry slide for another day. If you're taking the kids to a movie, leave the dishes soaking in the sink. If a child is sick and needs extra care, ask a friend to take your place at the PTA committee meeting. It's common sense, but a parent's guilt can be the enemy of common sense. Maybe what you have to do is allow for a different mind-set—one that gives permission to let some things go. For example, when I was growing up, my mother taught me that it was a hard and fast rule *never* to leave the house without first making the bed. I still remember how tremendously liberating it was for me, after I had become a parent, to decide it was okay to walk out the door with the beds unmade. When you think of all the serious problems in the world, unmade beds and toys strewn around the house really don't qualify as cardinal sins. In fact, do they really matter at all?

One useful suggestion is to separate "good" guilt from "bad" guilt. As Susan Ginsberg described it in her newsletter, *Work and Family*

Life, "Good guilt is the kind that motivates you to make constructive changes or to recognize that something you did or said was out of line or hurtful. Bad guilt, which I would unscientifically estimate accounts for 99 percent of what most parents feel—stems from thinking that the answer to the question 'Can you do it all?' should be '*Yes.*' "

Feelings of doubt, disappointment, and regret can be very uncomfortable—especially since parents usually try so hard to do the "right" thing. But these emotions are normal and acceptable. Of course, you're going to feel disappointed if you miss your daughter's dance recital. But that's different from blaming yourself for something over which you have no control—especially when it probably doesn't matter much in the scheme of things. I still remember how terrible I felt when I was twenty minutes late to my son Eric's first-grade spring play. I missed his performance as a toy soldier and suffered guilt pangs for days. Of course, Eric doesn't even remember being *in* the play, much less my not being there.

❧ *2. Equalize the parenting.*

It's obvious that women who have an equal parenting partnership with their husbands are going to be under less stress. But how can you make that happen? Nearly every mother I know finds that the primary responsibility for the kids is hers. Mothers really know the daily mundane details of everyday routine events—when the doctor's appointments are, the date of the school play, the presents to get for birthday parties and whose turn it is to host a play date.

Dads can seem like bumbling sidekicks. It's not a very positive scenario, and it can make fathers feel inept or left out. As Ron Taffel put it in his book, *Why Parents Disagree,* "The less men participate in the family network, the more isolated they are from the fabric of everyday life. In this way, the 'Mom's responsible' paradigm becomes self-perpetuating—and parental tension is inevitable. Men *know* that they're out of the loop. 'The phone rings all night,' they tell me, 'and ninety-nine percent of the calls are for *her!*' "

So, if this is an issue in your household, how *do* you help your husband become more a part of the daily routine? One thing you can do is talk with your spouse about this imbalance, preferably when you're calm. At times, it's a good idea to remind Dad how important he is. You might say something like, "You know, your opinions are very important to her. She takes things much more seriously when they come from you." When I give a speech to a group that includes fathers, I always make a point of addressing them and saying, "You probably don't even realize how necessary you are to your children's well-being and self-image, since so much of the parenting talk seems to be addressed to mothers." I notice men in the audience nodding their heads in agreement.

If you want your husband to get more involved, don't sabotage his efforts with comments like:

"How could you let her eat that?"

"Why didn't you remind him to put away his things?"

"I can't believe you let her wear that!"

"How come the kids are still up?"

It's not very motivating for dads to share the parenting responsibilities if they're always being told they can't do the job as effectively as you.

3. Be their parent, not their friend.

Accept the fact that your kids won't be thrilled with all of your rules and limits. If you spend too much time trying to please them, you're falling into what I call the happiness trap.

I always remind parents that they are the party poopers of their children's lives. "You are their parents, *not* their grandparents!" Your job as a parent usually boils down to saying no when your kids want you to say yes. Children won't always be delighted with you when you enforce limits.

Never ask your kids for permission to do what needs to be done. If you ask, "Is it okay if Mommy leaves for work now?" you're bound to be met with a resounding "No!" Less direct but equally ineffective is "Mommy's leaving now . . . okayyy?" Don't say, "If you promise not to cry when Mommy leaves, I'll bring you a present." Or, "Be good and we'll go out for a special treat tonight." Emotional blackmail sets a precedent. You keep having to pay, and some kids will up the ante. Even asking when you need their compliance can backfire, as in, "Would you mind taking out the garbage?" Instead, be firm and clear about what needs to happen, and keep it short: "Time for dinner." "Coats on." "In the car." "Shoes." "Let's go." "Randy, the garbage."

✌ 4. Simplify when possible.

Dr. Haim Ginott once said, "Efficiency is the enemy of childhood," and truer words were never spoken! I've almost never met a parent who loved the morning rush or who thoroughly enjoyed the combination of dinner, homework, bath, and bedtime. Kids have fabulous built-in radar for pushing your buttons at the worst possible times. Try telling a three-year-old, "Honey, could we discuss your doll's missing arm later when we're not on our way out the door?" Good luck. And don't be surprised if your first grader waits until the lights are out to call you back into the room to tell you she forgot that you're supposed to supply the goodies for snacktime the next day.

Mornings and evenings will cure you of the idea that perfection is ever achievable, especially with two or more who have different needs, schedules, and ages. Instead, they'll probably test your sanity. What helps is to find those areas where you *can* be efficient. For example, if it's possible, get ready the night before: clothes laid out, school lunches packed, table set for breakfast, knapsacks organized and set by the front door, shoes located. The shoes are particularly important. Shoes seem to have a life of their own in the morning, unless they are secured in a predetermined spot. And they're the one item of clothing that must be found. Why else would they be so easy to lose?

Another way to make life simpler with young children is to child-proof your home. The mother of very active twin toddlers realized that "ninety percent of my day was devoted to following them around, closing doors, putting objects out of reach, and moving them bodily out of danger's way. Every other word out of my mouth was 'No!' or 'Don't.' I

finally thought, this is silly. I loved the way my living room was deco-
rated, but it definitely wasn't toddler proof. So, I gave up the knick-
knacks, got rid of the decorative objects, put a soft mat over the brick
fireplace surface, moved the lamp, and put plastic caps over the electri-
cal outlets. Now I feel less antsy about letting the kids be in there
alone. And I have more down time."

🍂 5. Start the day in an upbeat way.

Try starting the day off with a smile and a cheerful "Good morning!"
You may not feel very cheerful or animated, but I guarantee you'll get
more cooperation if you do wakeup calls cheerfully instead of barking,
"Get your lazy butt out of bed this minute!" If you have a child who's a
real sleepyhead, always needing to be reawakened several times before
he or she finally gets up, don't fight it. Instead, make a "snooze"
agreement: After the first call, the child is allowed to go back to sleep
for five or ten minutes. But the second call is final. Another idea is to
provide the child with an alarm clock that has a snooze button and let
her take responsibility for getting herself up.

Avoid arguments about what to wear. If your five-year-old prefers
paisley pants with a checkered blouse and black knee socks, try not to
cringe. And by all means, don't let your mind wander to what the
teacher might be saying about *you*. If you've ever visited a kindergarten
class, you'll know that on some days it looks like a rummage sale.

Many parents tell me that breakfast is one of the most trying times
of the day. For some reason, kids love to argue about cereal. It's a law of
nature that the most coveted cereal is in the box that's almost empty.
Avoid these battles by making breakfast decisions the night before so
you can determine if there's enough cereal for two or three or however
many cereal eaters you have. One parent has a rule: "If there aren't
enough Cheerios for two, nobody gets Cheerios." Another parent had a
slightly different rule: "If there aren't enough Cheerios for two, *I* get the
Cheerios."

Simplify breakfast. We've all had it hammered home to us that
breakfast is the most important meal of the day, but it's not always

possible to get everyone through a healthy breakfast on time. One mother told me somewhat guiltily, "We were so late the other morning that I gave my son one of my Slimfast diet bars to eat in the car." Actually, eating in the car isn't such a terrible idea. A bag of Fingos (cereal you can eat with your hands), a carton of milk or juice with a straw, an apple, a granola bar, a bagel—there are plenty of car-friendly foods.

Establish a routine and display it for all to see. Meryl created a cheerful poster for her three-year-old twins that showed the morning routine in words and pictures.

Good Morning School Day

1. Wake up
2. Bathroom
3. Get dressed
4. Breakfast
5. Teeth
6. Shoes on
7. Brush hair
8. Jackets
9. Out the door—leave for school
   Bye-bye

"The Good Morning chart gave the boys a structure they could follow, and it worked most of the time," Meryl said. "It made us all feel a little more upbeat about the mornings."

Of course, nothing is foolproof. When I discussed these techniques in one of my groups, one mother immediately piped up, "Having a routine is fine. It helps. But you're not mentioning the little bombs your kids set off unexpectedly. When one says to the other, 'Gee, you look ugly in that shirt.' And the other one says, 'Well, I won't wear it.' And he comes running to you: 'Where's my blue shirt, the one with the

Snoopy?' And your routine is blown. You laid out the clothes the night before, everything's organized, but so what? Now we're searching high and low for the Snoopy shirt and the bus is due in five minutes."

"Well," I said, "obviously, you can't prepare for every inevitability. But no one says you have to drop everything and spend fifteen minutes searching for a shirt. You're allowed to say, 'Time's up. The bus is coming. You can wear the Snoopy shirt tomorrow.' It doesn't always work, but you can try not to get sucked into the tornado."

❧ 6. Don't sweat the small stuff.

It's okay to lower your standards. Don't spend so much time trying to do what's impossible. As the comedian Phyllis Diller once said, "Cleaning your house while your children are still young is like shoveling the sidewalk before it stops snowing." Can you let go of the need to be Supermom? I actually know a woman, the mother of five, who doesn't even worry about cleaning her house before guests come. I really admire her. She shrugs and says, "If people don't accept that a house with five kids is going to be a mess, I don't want them as friends."

Another way to make life easier with more than one is to lower your standards at night. It's not surprising that kids can be so uncooperative in the evenings. Evenings can be such a grind: Do your homework, eat your broccoli, take a bath, brush your teeth—oops, you ate a cookie, brush your teeth again—lights out. It's not much fun for you, either. One mother said she felt so much like a traffic cop that she ought to be wearing a whistle around her neck. Everyone is tired at the end of the day, and sometimes it's better to forgo a bath, cheat on the chores, or order takeout food. If you're flexible some of the time, it's easier to encourage cooperation at other times. For example, you might make a deal: "I'll tell you what, we'll skip the bath tonight so we can relax and watch that animal special on TV. But tomorrow night we'll really have to scrub. What do you say?"

You need to set priorities. How important are dust bunnies under the bed compared to tickle time on top of the bed? What's the worst thing that ever happened to an unwashed dish? Is it really a sin to wear day-old underwear? Go to school in wrinkled clothing? And do your kids really need a hot meal every single evening?

Another helpful question to ask yourself is "Will this matter a week from now?" We can feel terrible about things that are quickly forgotten. In the heat of the moment, we tend to confuse a mishap with a tragedy. If only we could save our guilt for the really important things—or at least the things we can control.

❧ *7. Don't take the blame.*

Try to ignore the people in your life who are only too happy to drip a little poison on your plate—"Is she *your* daughter?" "Do your kids *always* dress like that?" "Doesn't she have a hat?" You have to get rid of the poison before you eat it—or before it eats you. Your own mother or mother-in-law might be the worst culprit—"You're feeding them *that*?" Stand your ground and set your priorities.

Try not to get sucked into the blame-the-parent mentality.

Sandy, whose brood of five kept her on her toes at all times, remarked, "Isn't it funny that when your child does well, people give the child credit—as they should. But when a child misbehaves, who gets the blame? Mom!"

I recognized this as the age-old BTP syndrome: Blame the Parent. The only way out is to do some reality testing. Ask yourself if the judgment is fair. When you're feeling like a "bad" parent because you were the only one to miss the kindergarten pageant (impossibly scheduled for eleven o'clock when you were at the office), ask yourself, "Is this something I can control or change?" If not, don't let it torment you. If your job or the demands of an infant don't allow you to attend your son's baseball game, can you accept the fact that it's out of your hands?

It does seem sad but true that the blame always comes home to roost in the parent's lap—but not the praise. When your child is doing great, you hear, "What a wonderful *child*." When he's acting like a real pain, you hear, "What a terrible *parent*." And not only do you hear it from outsiders (most vocally from people who have never had children themselves), but you hear it in your own head, as well. Try not to accept such negative messages the next time your child throws a rubber-kneed sit-down strike in the supermarket or fidgets and whines during a family dinner with your in-laws.

❧ *8. Be inventive.*

One mother who fretted, "If I have to read the Berenstain Bears one more time, I'm going to lose it," came up with the idea of tape recording the books she had no patience for so her kids could listen to them whenever they wanted to. That's a good example of using creativity to release yourself from some of the most tedious obligations of parenting. (Taping stories, songs, and poems is also a wonderful strategy when you go away without the children.)

❧ *9. Call a time-out.*

This is a period when everybody takes a nap or has a quiet time alone. Establish a set period every day that's defined as a quiet time for the whole family. The kids go to their rooms, you go to yours. No talking, complaining, demands, or questions until the alarm or timer goes off. Although small children tend to be suspicious that nap times are simply your way of getting rid of them so you can have some serious fun (they're never tired!), impress upon them that everyone needs a break for rest and rejuvenation, even mommies and daddies. One mother set up a "battery recharge" period for her eight- and five-year-old sons. She told them, "We're not Energizer bunnies! We can't keep going and going without a break." A single father who worked at home found that the period between four and five in the afternoon was when most of the fighting occurred. He told his kids, "From now on, this hour is for time alone. You don't have to sleep or rest, but you have to be alone." He found that by five o'clock everyone was in a much better mood, including him, and the evenings went more smoothly.

🐾 *10. Encourage your kids to take care of* you.

Have you ever tried asking your kids to baby you? As an occasional strategy it really works. Cathy stumbled on the technique by accident on a day when she was really exhausted. "My seven-year-old was shooting spitballs out of a straw, his five-year-old sister was whining, 'I'm hungry!' and I was feeling like I wanted to walk out the front door and keep going. It was ninety degrees, the air-conditioning was on the blink, and little driblets of sweat were dripping off my chin. I flopped down on the couch and started moaning, 'Oh, poor me, poor me, I have just had it up to *here*.' The kids stopped what they were doing and came over and started stroking me. They weren't used to Mommy whining. I said, 'Please, can someone get me a drink of water with ice? I'm soooo hot.' They raced into the kitchen and after much clattering returned with a big glass of ice water, which they fed me through the spitball straw. It was a lovely switch, the kids taking care of me! And not only did I feel more loving toward them, they felt good about themselves for helping out."

🐾 *11. Don't put yourself last.*

Perhaps one reason why so many mothers feel overwhelmed by their multiple roles is simply that they have little opportunity to stoke their own fires. They put everything and everyone else before themselves, thinking, "I can wait. My needs are not that important. My kids come first. My job comes first. My husband comes first." And then they find themselves wondering, "Wait a minute. When do I ever get time for myself?"

Mothers often remark that parenting is a twenty-four-hour-a-day job, and in some respects this is true. But it's impossible to keep giving, giving, giving without getting a break—not just for your sake, but for your kids' sake as well.

Carol, a busy mother of three who runs a business out of her home, finds her best time is early in the morning. "I get up earlier than everyone else and that's the space in my day that's totally quiet when I can indulge myself. I go for a walk or make a list of things I want to accomplish that day, or I just sit in the kitchen and drink my coffee in peace. Having this time just for me makes it easier to move into the day without a lump of stress in my stomach."

Lee, a mother of two who has a demanding full-time job, manages to find her "break" when she's commuting. "I don't really have any other time for myself," she said. "It's always either work or my children, and when the kids fall asleep, I fall asleep right after them because I'm so tired. But I do have my commuting time. When I'm driving to and from work, that's the one time in the day when I'm alone. Nobody is bothering me or asking me for things. It's my special time to just think or listen to books on tape and enjoy the fact that no one can make demands on me."

It's good for children to see their parents taking care of their own needs. Even though kids are by nature egocentric and don't really care most of the time if you're tired or rushed or feeling down, in the long run you'll set a positive example by attending to your own needs. Nan, a mother in my workshop, told the group how she swallowed her guilt and decided to do something for herself. "I went to play tennis, and the court has a baby-sitting service for a dollar an hour. When I dropped off the kids, they were outraged. They couldn't believe I was leaving them to play tennis! My daughter started whining, 'I want to be with you.' I was very straightforward with them. I said, 'You have your friends and I have mine, and I'm going to play with *my* friends for an hour.' And that was it. They didn't like it, but it felt good to help them realize that mommies get to play too—that we're not just mommy machines."

Remember What Matters

While we're spending time and energy worrying about all the little pieces that aren't fitting together in our "perfect family" puzzle, we can forget what's really important. It seems so obvious, yet I find we have to be continually reminded to look at the big picture of our lives. Recently, Louise, a parent in my workshop group, helped all of us when she shared the painful way she gained perspective. Louise told the group that last year she'd been diagnosed with ovarian cancer, and although she's in remission, the confrontation with mortality changed everything.

"Now, I don't care if the homework doesn't always get done," she said. "I'm not so picky anymore about the house being clean. Those things just aren't important." As we listened to Louise, every parent in the room felt deeply shaken. We were all saddened that Louise's perspective was so hard earned. But it gave us an opportunity to look at ourselves, too. In her simple and direct way, Louise helped to remind us all that what we really cared about was these precious human beings, our children. Everything else could wait.

Chapter 4

Sibling Wars without End

You should never pick on your sister when she has a baseball bat in her hands.

—Joel, age twelve, as quoted in
Wit and Wisdom from the Peanut Butter Gang

"Mommy, Mommy, Greg pushed me."

"You bumped me first."

"Liar!"

"You kids stop that right now or I'm coming in there."

"Aieee! Mommy!"

"I'm warning you."

"Owwwww . . ."

"Okay, that does it. You're in trouble now."

Does this sound like your household? Do you feel as if you live in a seething cauldron of sibling unrest? Join the club! It's the number one topic among parents of more than one: what to do about the fighting, jealousy, squabbling, picking on each other, pushing, pinching, and name calling.

When I ask parents why they decided to have more than one child, the most common answer is that they did it for the sake of their first child—to give him or her the "gift" of a sibling. I often hear adults who were only children themselves talking about how lonely it was to grow up without brothers and sisters, and how much they longed for a sibling. They are convinced that it will mean a lot to their own children to have sibling companions.

But parents are almost always shocked when the "gift" isn't welcome—when their children act more like enemies than friends, when the bickering and jealousy and rivalry are constants rather than the loving companionship they had hoped for.

One of my favorite stories about sibling rivalry was told by the writer Louise Bates Ames, a child development expert from the Gesell Institute. She described a woman who was pregnant with her second child. One day, her three-year-old son kept poking her belly harder and harder. While restraining him, she thought to ask, "Are you trying to say something to the baby?"

"Yeah," he replied. "Come on out and fight."

We don't like it, but sibling battles are a fact of life. It is one of the more upsetting aspects of parenting to see your kids bickering and being antagonistic toward one another. But if it is the nature of adults to long for peace, it is the nature of children to upset domestic tranquillity.

Kids Fight over the Darnedest Things

What do siblings fight about? The short answer is everything and nothing. Parents I've interviewed on the subject frequently used the words "silly things" when asked what their children fought about. These included: who sits where (at home and in the car), what TV programs to watch, who holds the remote control, who gets to choose the snack, who plays with which toy, who picks the movie, who turns on the light, who gets to lie on Mommy's pillow, which one gets into the car first—as well as squabbles over real and imagined inequities. It drives parents crazy!

The parents I surveyed had plenty to say about why their kids fight. Many of their comments will probably sound familiar:

- "Fairness in a zillion forms—size and number of toys, number of play dates in a week, length of school day, and so on.

My six-year-old is obsessed with everything being equal with the four-year-old."

- "Often, I never know what they're fighting about. One of them will just come indoors saying, 'He pushed me.' Or 'She made a face at me.' Or 'He's bothering me.' The other day I had to laugh. It was, 'She breathed on me!'"

- "Everything! If they don't have something specific to fight about, they just tease and harass each other. Like last night, they were arguing about whose blue coat was bluer!"

- "My son says the only time he fights with his older sister is when she won't play with him. He has a limitless passion for playing games and make-believe with her, and she, as the older one, gets bored. So, typically, she will shut him out of her room and he will rage and mope."

- "Who gets to turn off the television. Who gets to turn on the light. Who gets to stand on the stool at the bathroom sink. Also, they fight when one splashes the other in the bathtub, when one hurts the other, when one won't play a game that the other wants to play, or when they both want to play the same game—alone!"

- "Stupid things! Any little scrap of paper that one picks up, the other will suddenly covet it. 'He's sitting in my chair.' 'How come she's not picking up when I have to?' '*I* wanted to open the front door.' I'm convinced they mostly fight to get my attention, and they do get it since it's so hard to ignore their squabbling."

One mother told me that her children used to argue loudly and passionately about the temperature at which water boiled in the mountains. "They fought about it so frequently that it became a family joke. The question never got resolved, so I decided that they just liked to fight about it."

The fact is, kids fight about anything and everything simply because it's the fighting itself, not its content, that holds endless appeal. Parents forget that fighting can be fun, and it's never boring. They worry that sibling fights are a grim precursor to a lifetime of hatred. Sometimes they can't believe these are really their children. "I'm always thinking, I'm not supposed to have these kids," said Zoe, a gentle, soft-spoken young mother of two very aggressive boys. "How can these be my kids? I'm such a pacifist, and I hate noise and disorder. I half believe my boys came from the cabbage patch—or, more likely, the planet Jupiter!"

When Fighting Turns Mean

Parents usually grow accustomed to a certain amount of bickering and fighting among their children. They don't like it, but they realize it comes with the territory. Deliberate meanness is another matter. In one of my workshops, Carla painfully related how her eleven-year-old son behaved in ways that were downright cruel toward his six-year-old sister. "It's really hard to watch her being tortured by him," she said. "She absolutely worships the ground he walks on, and he daily proclaims his hatred of her. He crushes her with his comments and bullies her into giving him things. He complains that we favor her, and I guess we do because she's so cheerful and he's so dour. I said to him, 'We'll favor you when you start acting like your sister.' I shouldn't have said that, I guess, but I was just so frustrated."

I asked Carla if she intervened when her son picked on his sister.

"It's hard not to," she admitted. "My daughter is so sweet and compliant. I feel the need to protect her. And also to teach her not to be a victim, to be stronger and stick up for herself."

I asked Carla to give us an example.

"Okay. She needed a lightbulb for her newest prize toy, her Easy Bake Oven. And he manipulated her. He said, 'I'll give you a lightbulb from my room, but you have to let me play with the oven first.' And she was willing to give up the pleasure of being the first to use her oven. Then ironically, he needed the same kind of lightbulb later in the week and she said, 'I'll go get the one you gave me.' And she gave it back to him expecting to be allowed to play. Then he took the bulb for himself and shut her out of his room. She was devastated. And this happens time after time."

"What did you do?" I asked.

"My first instinct was to yell at him for being so cruel and selfish. That's usually what I do. But for a change, I tried a different approach. I said to Julia, 'Listen, you know you and your brother are different. He's not willing to share as much as you are. Let's give him some space.' He was surprised to hear me tell her that, but I felt really good about my response. Ordinarily, I would have taken her side and yelled at him."

"Good for you," I said encouragingly. "You saw it from his point of view. That's a start."

Carla grimaced. "Not really. It was like he wasn't able to give up being mean to her. I felt as though he was egging me on to yell at him."

I laughed. "He probably was. You see, by intervening, you're trying to make it better for her. And he's determined not to allow you to do that. Let me suggest another approach. I think you have the right idea about empowering your daughter. The next time she complains to you about him, try saying, 'Yes, it must be frustrating. Gosh, your brother sure does know how to upset you. Do you really want to play with him when he's being mean to you? Would you rather do something else? You know, you don't have to be around him when he's not being nice to you.' Give her some options and show her that she doesn't have to stay and be a victim."

Margo told the workshop group how frustrated she was by the nastiness of fourteen-year-old Carrie toward seven-year-old Emma. In large part, she blamed the age span. "Carrie is such a prickly teenager, and Emma is such an agreeable little girl, it's like they're on different wavelengths," Margo said. "They don't speak the same language. Carrie likes to be sarcastic, dry, and rude. Sometimes she's very funny, but it's teenage talk and Emma doesn't like being on the receiving end of Carrie's jibes."

"For example?" I asked.

"The other night Emma was eating spaghetti, and she was having so much fun slurping the noodles. She said, 'Look, Mom, look how I eat spaghetti!' And Carrie said with a loud stage whisper—loud enough for

Emma to hear—'You look good eating worms, Emma. That's what you should be eating—worms, red and white worms.' Emma was crushed, but Carrie thought it was a riot."

Although she was annoyed by Carrie's behavior, Margo thought about how she could best approach her older daughter to gain her cooperation without sermonizing and engendering resistance. Margo understood that teenagers need a certain amount of space to be gross and outrageous. It's the nature of the beast! But by planning ahead of time what she would say, Margo was able to find a way to bring out Carrie's basically loving nature:

MARGO: Can I talk to you for a minute?

CARRIE: What's up?

MARGO: It's about Emma. I wanted you to know that she's bringing her class photos home today.

CARRIE: So? What does that have to do with me?

MARGO: Well, you know Emma. She thinks your opinion is the only one that counts. She looks up to you and worships the ground you walk on. So, I was thinking, maybe you could just chill a little with the jokes and critical remarks.

CARRIE: (suddenly being very adult) Okay, Ma. I hear you.

When Emma came home, Carrie made a big production about the school pictures. "You look so pretty, Emma! Can I have one for my room?" Emma just glowed. Later, Margo took Carrie aside.

MARGO: You really made Emma feel good. That was so sensitive of you. I really appreciate it.

CARRIE: (pleased) No sweat, Mom.

Fighting can turn serious as children get older. Preteens and teens can be deliberately cruel, zeroing in on a sibling's greatest vulnerability. Fran, the mother of a fourteen-year-old daughter and a sixteen-year-old son, told how agonizing it was for her to listen to the hurtful words that passed between her children. She gave an example:

KEVIN: You've got such a big butt. You and your fat rear end, I can see it coming for miles.

JODIE: Yeah, well at least a pimple factory didn't explode on my face. Zit city!

Fran sighed. "The other day it made me so miserable that I was beside myself. I choked out, 'I could just cry hearing the both of you.' They turned and looked at me as if I'd gone mad."

Fran told me that what upset her the most was hearing Kevin harangue Jodie about her weight. "I don't want her to start thinking she's fat. That's such a big deal for a girl. I want her self-esteem to be strong enough so that she doesn't get into that diet craziness."

No parent can hear those kinds of insults and remain indifferent. "If you really believe the words are damaging, or the kids are taking them to heart, you need to take a stand," I told Fran. "Even if you have to say it a thousand times, your values need to be firmly reinforced: 'In this house, there will be no hurting—physical or emotional.' "

However, I also suggested to Fran that although she has to step in and discourage this kind of name calling, she might also want to consider just how seriously Jodie was taking her brother's taunts. "It sounds horrible to you because you can't imagine speaking that way to your daughter—or to anyone, for that matter," I said. "And I'm not condoning it. I strongly believe that we have to let our children know this kind of insulting is 'below the belt.' However, Jodie sounds like she has a pretty good handle on things. She's not withering away when her brother insults her. She's fighting back. So, I don't think you necessarily have to worry about her self-esteem unless she takes his taunting seriously. If that's the case, you have to make your position loud and clear."

Trying to teach siblings to express anger, irritation, annoyance, or resentment toward one another without cruelty can be an exhausting and discouraging process. But we have to keep hammering away. It's one of the most valuable lessons we can teach our children.

Peggy instituted a clear rule to cut down on the verbal insults between her two boys. "I tell them they can dislike each other, they can hate each other, but they need to rein in their hurtful words. I don't want to hear them. I know I can't control much of what they say to each other when they're out of earshot, but at least I can insist upon my values when they're in my presence."

Why Do Kids Pick on Each Other?

Parents don't always consider that when an older child picks on a younger one, it may be because he or she is feeling left out, ignored, unheard. If there seems to be a constant pattern of insults, it may help to explore what's causing one sibling to attack another. One mother told me that her thirteen-year-old son was always complaining about his five-year-old sister. "He thinks she gets away with murder," this mother said wearily. "But I constantly tell him, 'Come on, she's only five!' "

"You believe he should be more tolerant of her because he's so much older," I said.

"I certainly do. A five-year-old is obviously going to have more needs than a thirteen-year-old," she replied.

"Yes, in a practical sense that's true," I said. "But your son doesn't see that. He might be more cooperative if you try responding to his feelings with empathy rather than just reiterating the fact that she's younger. Perhaps you could say to him, 'You feel I'm not strict enough with her? What do you wish I did differently?' Then listen to him without criticism and allow him to try to specify his objections. Perhaps he does have some legitimate complaints."

One father asked his preadolescent son what made him so impatient with his younger sister. The boy replied, "She comes into my room when I'm not home and messes up my things." This was more specific than "She's such a brat." It gave Dad a basis for offering support: "Oh, I can see why that would bug you. What can we do to make your room an off-limits zone when you're out of the house?"

Here's where it can be powerful to acknowledge feelings while at the same time not permitting unacceptable behavior. If one of your children crosses the line, be direct. Say, "I can see why you'd be furious that Jen wrecked your puzzle. But I'm not going to let you hurt her. My job as a parent is to make sure that everyone in this house feels safe."

To Intervene or Not to Intervene

Most of the people I interviewed said that their own parents usually intervened in their sibling fights. Often, they recalled these interventions as being unwelcome, unfair, insulting or just completely ineffective. Betsy, one of four, recalled one incident vividly. "I was angry with my younger sister and was rubbing leaves in her hair as we wrestled. My father grabbed me and really roughed me up in the leaves and said, 'There, how do you like that!' I was furious at him and thought how I'd get back at my sister later when he wasn't around. And I did, too."

Ruth told one of my workshop groups about a tussle between her six-year-old daughter and her three-year-old son. "They don't fight much, but I happened to look up just as Lynda was whapping Gregory really hard on the chest. And I yelled, 'Lynda, how can you do that? Stop it right now!' They both looked up at me. Little Gregory was positively disgusted. He said, 'Mommy, you're stupid.' I don't appreciate being called stupid, and I let him know it. But I did appreciate the fact that he was defending his sister. He neither wanted nor needed my intervention."

To intervene or not to intervene—that is the question parents most often ask. One mother, who had a firm rule about not intervening when her kids quarreled, described how she had trained herself to tune out everything but serious fights. One day her husband shouted at her, "Are you deaf?" She shouted back, "Yes!"

She told me, "I find that I'm much happier and my kids seem to fight less now that I stay out of it."

I encourage parents to stay out of the middle unless the fighting is violent or deliberately cruel. Often, the main reason kids fight is because they want your attention. They'll fight because they're bored and want to get you involved in the middle. They'll yell, "Mommeee, he called me a name!" since it's always fun to try to get a sibling in trouble. We know that kids can't bear too much tranquillity. And if you run into the room to intervene every time there's a fight, they've accomplished their goal of getting you involved, hoping you'll accuse one and stick up for the other.

Therefore, when one child poses as a victim in order to get a sibling punished, and you go along, exonerating one and chastising the other, be prepared for another fight to erupt very soon after. You can be sure that the child you reprimanded will find a way to even the score. The parent who intervenes in every conflict will inevitably discover that the conflicts multiply in proportion to the number of interventions. And the most futile question in the world is "Who started it?"

However, when the fighting gets physical or emotionally hurtful, you do have to intervene. The question is, how can your intervention help them solve the problem instead of escalating it or making things worse by starting another fight as soon as your back is turned? Yelling at your kids rarely works, especially when they're busy yelling at each other. It just raises the noise level. But trying to get them to figure out solutions is a helpful way of intervening. One mother shared this dialogue of her attempt to help her son stop hitting his brother.

MOM: David, hitting is not allowed in our house.

DAVID: But Lyle makes me so mad. He just wrecked my Erector set building. I could kill him! It took me hours to do.

MOM: I can see why you'd be furious.

DAVID: You would be, too.

MOM: Did you tell him how angry you are?

DAVID: Yeah, I tell him, but he doesn't listen.

MOM: Can you think of another way besides hitting to keep
           Lyle out of your stuff?

DAVID: Yeah. Keeping him out of my room.

MOM: How will you do that?

DAVID: I'll put a big sign on my door: Keep Out!

MOM: That's an idea. Why don't you try it. But no hitting.

Rather than interfering by taking sides or punishing, you can often use sibling fights as a chance to teach kids problem solving. This is one method many of my workshop parents have tried successfully. When the kids are fighting and come to you to complain about who did what to whom, try this. Ask each child to tell his or her side of the story, but make it clear that you'll listen only as long as each child is allowed to talk without being interrupted. After each has taken his turn, ask the other to say what they heard their sibling saying. Then help them brainstorm solutions. Some siblings are willing to write down where the injustice lay, according to their perception. Then, with a parent acting as impartial arbitrator, they can compare versions. We'll talk more about these techniques later in the chapter.

When Your Spouse Gets into the Act

There's a popular myth that parents should always present a united front when it comes to discipline. People are surprised and angry when that doesn't happen. But when you think about it, it isn't even realistic to expect you and your spouse to agree about discipline. After all, you were raised in different families with different disciplinary styles— permissive versus authoritarian, demonstrative versus distant, easygoing versus strict. If either of you was an only child, there was no model at all for dealing with sibling fights. If you are like most parents, you'll probably disagree with each other over many issues. However, that doesn't mean you have to constantly fight with each other over whose method is best.

First, be aware that kids are incredibly adept at sensing weakness in the parental front. They will divide and conquer if you let them. Try to agree on your rules in advance, and then stick to them.

Jane and Mark had very different styles when it came to handling disputes. Jane, who came from a large family where noisy battles were the norm, tended to let the kids work out their own problems. If it got too noisy, she put on her Walkman and went on about her business. This drove Mark crazy. When he was growing up, his parents had always intervened when he and his sister argued. They didn't tolerate noise. Because they had such different ideas about what was right, Jane and Mark often ended up yelling at each other while their kids stood by and watched anxiously.

I suggested to them that they try to work out a compromise that they could both live with. "Mark," I said, "you hate the noise, and I don't blame you. Everyone wants a little peace and quiet sometimes. Why don't you try this. The next time your kids start bickering, set the kitchen timer to four minutes. If they're still arguing when the timer goes off, then step in. But resist the urge to intervene before that."

Mark agreed. To his surprise, he discovered that the arguments rarely lasted the full four minutes. "It always seemed like they went at it for hours," he said, still somewhat amazed. "But I guess it only *felt* like hours."

I also urge parents to decide in advance what are the nonnegotiable rules in the family they can both agree on. Then they need to be firm and consistent. When Dad says, "Ask your mother," that is his way of saying, "I give up." Children have to know that they're going to get the same answer from both parents. That way they are discouraged from playing off one parent against the other. If you do disagree with your spouse's decision (and you probably will at times), don't override him in front of the kids. But it's fine to say, "Dad and I don't feel the same way about that. We'll discuss it and get back to you." This teaches children that disagreements can lead to negotiation and compromise.

Sharon was pretty relaxed about grades, but her husband Kevin was very strict—and the kids knew it. When Jack, their youngest, brought home a D in math, he headed straight for his mother—naturally!

JACK: Please don't tell Dad. He'll freak out!

MOM: Dad cares a great deal about your grades. Would you rather tell him yourself?

This mother admitted that it was difficult to resist the urge to keep the poor report card grade from Dad. She was tempted to let Jack know she thought his father was too strict. Certainly, Jack would have felt relieved for the moment. But she had made a prior agreement with her husband that despite their different attitudes about schoolwork, they would strive for common ground and not sabotage each other's efforts by keeping secrets.

Parents can present a model of fighting fair to their children. Your kids are going to watch you for signs of how to behave. If you typically respond to disagreements with name-calling or put-downs, that's the lesson your kids are going to learn. This point came home to Lynn during this discussion with her son, Charlie:

CHARLIE: Daddy's a jerk!

LYNN: That's a terrible thing to say.

CHARLIE: Well, it's true. He's a jerk.

LYNN: I don't like you to talk that way about your father.

CHARLIE: I don't care, he *is* a jerk.

Finally, not knowing what else to say, Lynn asked Charlie:

LYNN: Charlie, what *is* a jerk, anyway?

CHARLIE: That's easy. It's what Daddy calls everybody when we're driving in the car.

If you and your spouse find yourself loudly locking horns over discipline techniques, it might be useful to keep the following points in mind:

- Expect to disagree. You were brought up in different families with different ways of doing things.

- Don't let the kids divide and conquer. If Dad says no, there's no asking Mom, and vice versa.
- Don't contradict your spouse in front of the kids. If you have to fight it out, do it later when your children are out of earshot.
- Don't play the middle person. If your child complains to you about the other parent, encourage him to discuss it directly with your spouse.
- Don't try to convince your spouse that he or she is wrong or inept. Wait until you've cooled off and then talk about it calmly. (And remember how hard it is to change yourself, much less another person!)

Techniques for Coping with Sibling Rivalry

Okay, so by now you've probably accepted the fact that it's normal for kids to fight. But knowing that doesn't help when the decibel levels are about to burst your eardrums, and you just can't stand it anymore. Sometimes it's just not humanly possible to grit your teeth and bear it. Besides, it's important to teach children that there are alternatives to breaking the sound barrier or duking it out.

Over the years, many parents have offered good solutions for substituting confrontation with cooperation. These suggestions fall into five basic categories: Consequences, Clarification, Negotiation, Distraction, and Empowerment.

❧ *Consequences*

We must teach kids that actions have consequences. It's a lesson they'll need when they grow up and are tempted to mouth off at the boss!

I like the solution of one father who got fed up with his three kids fighting in the car. Most parents I know think driving in a car with children is the worst ordeal of all, maybe because children often behave like caged animals. But jumping, pushing, hitting, and yelling in the car can be dangerous as well as annoying, and this father instituted a strict policy: If the kids started fighting, he would drive the car to the side of the road and make everyone get out and run around the car five times—rain or shine, snow or sleet. It didn't take long for his kids to get the message and quiet down in the car. He took action without lecturing or using too many words. The kids hated those runs! Now, when they are talking loudly or beginning to hassle one another and Dad starts to slow down, they immediately plead, "No, Dad, we're okay. Keep going, please!"

Roberta, a mother who was very good at ignoring the noise most of the time, established a rule that went into effect if she had to raise her voice more than once. "My kids know that means we're going to have a 'monk dinner'—no talking. They hate that. You can practically see the words piling up in their throats waiting to spill out."

I like Barbara Coloroso's simple method for dealing with the consequences of hitting, as described in her fine book, *Kids Are Worth It:* "From the time my own children were quite young, they learned that if you hit, you sit. Hitting is not an appropriate way to handle conflict at any age. It doesn't solve anything, and only invites more hitting. In our home if you hit somebody, you sit in the rocker or in your room." Coloroso goes one step further. When the child says he's ready to return to the group, she asks him what he plans to do. "If he says he's not going to hit, we aren't quite there yet—that's not a positive plan; it's what he's not going to do. I want to know what he's planning to do instead of hitting. . . ." In this way, Coloroso teaches clear consequences and positive action as an alternative to hitting.

Consequences are an effective alternative to punishment. When you do impose consequences, however, be sure not to confuse them with bribery. Bribery is "If you're good, we'll have ice cream later." Whereas a positive consequence is offered *after* the fact: "You kids played so nicely today that I'm taking you out for ice cream."

❧ *Clarification*

Consider the number of times a day you find yourself saying things like:

"Settle down."

"Play nicely."

"Cut it out!"

"Be nice."

"Behave yourselves."

"Shape up."

"Stop bickering."

"Get busy."

If these admonitions are common to you, you've probably discovered how ineffective they are. Children respond best to clear, concise statements, not vague wails of frustration. Nonspecific commands like "Be nice" only elicit replies like, "I *am* being nice. He started it." And the response you get to "Cut it out" might well be "Cut *what* out?" or "We weren't doing anything."

Instead, try a more specific approach. Make impersonal, concrete statements about what you want. Don't expect it to work every time, but it will surely work more often than vague statements like, "You kids stop it!" Here's the way one mother used cool, concise descriptiveness with her sons:

MOM: Jim, the dishes belong in the dishwasher, not in the sink.

JIM: Those are Alan's dishes in the sink.

ALAN: They are not. You're the one who was eating ice cream.

JIM: Yeah, but what about the spaghetti? That one's yours.

ALAN: Prove it!

MOM: (examining the dishes in the sink) That's funny. These dishes don't have any names on them. But I want them put in the dishwasher before the TV goes on.

Your goal here is to solve a problem, not to play judge and jury. Nor can you force your kids to love each other. You can't legislate love. You can only encourage cooperation. Being descriptive is an effective way to avoid personalizing behavior—to let your kids know what you want or expect without barking commands or sounding like a marine sergeant.

🍂 *Negotiation*

"With six- and four-year-olds, I'm amazed at how well the 'You guys work it out' phrase works," said Shirley. "We use this a lot when choosing which bedtime story will be read first. I refuse to come into the room until they have reached a decision. In the car, I say, 'You must agree on who sits in the front seat before I open the door.' They might decide that one of them sits there on the way to the store and the other on the way home. But *they're* the ones who have worked out a solution, not me."

The advantage of teaching your kids to find solutions to their disputes is that it leaves you out of it. Face it, you don't really want to spend your days arbitrating silly debates about who gets the orange Popsicle and who gets the red one. Kids aren't as busy as you are. They have plenty of time and more at stake in dragging out these arguments.

Negotiation works best when things are relatively calm. Don't try it when your kids are going at each other's throats. But once you've restored relative calm, say, "We have this problem. What do you think we can do about it?"

Don't expect the negotiation to model a sedate corporate boardroom. That doesn't mean it can't lead to a satisfying conclusion. Vivian tried this approach in the aftermath of a particularly loud and angry battle between her nine-year-old daughter, Amy, and her seven-year-old son, Randy. By the time Vivian arrived on the scene, Amy was sobbing that Randy had pulled her hair, and Randy was yelling that Amy had changed the channel on the TV without asking. Vivian began by separating them and sending them to their rooms for a five-minute cooldown period. Then, over a snack at the table, they had this conversation:

VIVIAN: Do you mind if I take notes so we can get the story straight? (The kids looked surprised, but they nodded.) Okay, what happened in there?

(Both kids began to talk at once.)

VIVIAN: Whoa! Let's set a ground rule here. One person at a time, no interrupting. Who wants to go first?

RANDY: She started it. I was watching my program, and she came in the room and clicked it to something else.

AMY: Liar. You weren't even watching it. You were playing with your racing set.

RANDY: I was watching out of the corner of my eye.

VIVIAN: Mmmm, I see. And what happened next?

AMY: He pulled my hair.

RANDY: She wouldn't give me the remote.

VIVIAN: So you pulled her hair?

RANDY: Yeah, so she'd let go.

VIVIAN: Okay, let me go over the notes and see if I got this straight. Amy went in the room and switched the TV to a different channel. Amy says Randy wasn't watching it anyway. Randy says he was watching out of the corner of his eye. Then Randy tried to take the remote away from Amy and she wouldn't give it to him. So he pulled her hair. Is that about right?

(Both kids nodded.)

VIVIAN: What do you think we can do to solve this problem?

AMY: I think Randy should be punished because he isn't allowed to pull my hair.

RANDY: But you started it. You're not innocent!

VIVIAN: If I punish Randy, or punish both of you, will that solve the problem?

RANDY: No, because she could just do it again. We should make a rule.

VIVIAN: Okay. Like what?

RANDY: If the TV is on and someone is there, you should *ask* him if he's watching.

AMY: Oh, yeah, so you can lie. You'd say you were, even if you weren't.

RANDY: No, I wouldn't.

AMY: You would, too!

VIVIAN: Well, this doesn't sound like a solution you can agree upon. Any other ideas?

AMY: We could have days when we get to choose all the afternoon programs, and the other person can't argue. They have to ask permission if they want to watch something else.

VIVIAN: Randy, what do you think about that?

RANDY: It could work, but I don't trust her. She'll say it's her day even when it's not.

VIVIAN: I'll tell you what. Why don't you get the TV schedule and make a chart for one week. If it doesn't work, we'll try something else.

(Amy and Randy ran off to get the schedule, then spent an hour negotiating a plan for one week.)

Vivian admitted that she had to bite her lip to avoid interfering. "And," she added, "I really didn't want to take the time for this long discussion. I had other things to do. But I have to say, it paid off in the end. It wasn't a perfect solution, but it set the stage for a certain style of problem solving when disputes arise. Now I ask, 'Do we have to take this to the table?' And they know what I mean. I've found that they'd rather work it out themselves than take the time away from playing to have a long discussion around the table."

When you teach your kids to negotiate their differences you are accomplishing more than just settling immediate disputes. You are giving them an invaluable life skill—learning to look within themselves to problem solve, and getting them in the habit of compromising.

I know that some parents may be thinking, "My kids could *never* learn to negotiate. Forget it!" But you never know unless you try. Ellie, the mother of two young boys, was amazed when negotiation actually worked. "It was a typical scene," she told me. "I was reading them a bedtime story, and I had one boy on either side of me. For some reason, they decided that sitting on my *right* side was the preferred position— who knows why? And they were arguing about it. I was tired of the squabbling, so I just said, '*You* work it out. I'll be back in three minutes.' I left the room, never imagining that they would actually reach an agreement. But when I returned, lo and behold, they had figured out a strategy. My eldest would sit on the right and his brother would sit on his lap. I was astonished and delighted. I thought two people couldn't sit in one spot, but I was wrong!"

🐾 *Distraction*

Instead of trying to address the issue at hand—which sometimes leads to no resolution—help your kids get *off* the point. This works especially well with younger children who are more easily distracted. Instead of saying, "You kids stop bickering," say, "Let's call Grandma," or "Who wants to go to the park?" or "It's time for a snack," or "I'll bet no one can guess what we're having for lunch."

A great way of distracting kids from an argument is to use humor. Phyllis, the harried mother of two preteens and a preschooler, told my workshop parents about this idea. "My two older ones were going at it full force," she said, "and I was really fed up. But instead of shouting at them, which was my usual ineffective strategy, I entered the room and said, 'Kids, wait! I'm going to get my tape recorder so we can record this argument for posterity. It's a doozy!' Well, they stopped dead in their tracks and stared at me. They thought I'd gone crazy. As I plugged in the tape recorder and started to set it up, they couldn't believe their eyes. It was a diversion from their argument, and helped lighten things up. Hey, I figured if they kept fighting, I really would record it and play it back to their kids."

Another parent distracts children from fighting by having them keep their hands behind their backs and sit facing one another without touching. They always end up with a case of the giggles.

A variation on distraction is separation. Physically move the children apart. This is an effective strategy because more often than not kids hate to be separated—even when they've been viciously fighting. "Whenever my six-year-old twins can't stop bickering over a toy or the TV, I separate them," Shauna reported. "I say, 'Oh, I can see that you two don't want to play together, so each of you go to a different corner of the room and play by yourself. We'll set the timer for fifteen minutes.' This drives them nuts. Within minutes, they're sneaking glances at each other, whispering under their breath and inching out of their corners. Playing alone is like being sent to Siberia."

Time out should be viewed as a cool-down period, not a punishment. You might even say something like, "I can see you two are too upset to stay together. I'm going to help you to cool down. You obviously need a break from one another."

❧ *Empowerment*

Parents have an opportunity to help their kids gain something positive from their fights. One mother offered this dialogue as an example of how she tried to get her younger daughter to think before she reacted to her brother's teasing:

MELISSA: (upset and crying) Jonathan called me a baby.

MOM: Are you a baby?

MELISSA: No!

MOM: I agree. Just because he said it doesn't mean he's right. In fact, I noticed just today how well you folded your clothes. That's not the behavior of a baby! So, when your brother calls you a baby, I'm surprised you believe him.

This parent helped her child see that she didn't have to be the helpless victim of her brother's name calling. "I felt very pleased with that conversation," this mother said later. "I feel very strongly that little girls are too often encouraged to be sweet and submissive and accept the judgments of others, even when they're put-downs. I wanted to give

Melissa another way of handling negative labels so they didn't chip away at her self-esteem."

All parents need to be able to empower their kids. But they don't always know how to deliver the message. And sometimes the message gets confused.

My husband Sy and I learned with our sons that it's not always so simple. When Todd was a baby, we took great pains to impress upon Eric, our older son, that physical aggression of any kind would not be allowed. Being a very sensitive kid, Eric took the message to heart and learned his lesson well, refusing to hit or use physical aggression. But as Todd grew, it became clear that he was more physical than Eric. Without our realizing it, he was beating up his older brother, and Eric was just taking it. One day, Sy walked into the room and saw Todd throw a punch at Eric. Eric was just standing there with tears in his eyes. Without thinking, Sy said angrily, "Why don't you fight back?" Eric sobbed, "We're not supposed to hit." We realized that our "no hitting" message had been translated in Eric's mind to "I can't stand up for myself."

We realized that we had taught Eric not to hit, but, perhaps because Todd was younger, we had failed to emphasize the same message as strongly to him. We had to go back and make sure that *both* boys understood the "no hitting" rule, while making it clear that asserting themselves and refusing to be victims was okay. Sometimes the line between the two is very blurred. My own experience has given me a real appreciation of how difficult it is to explain to your children the difference between being self-confident and assertive and being a bully.

In our increasingly violent society, if we can help our children to protect themselves without being either a victim or a victimizer, we have given them an invaluable legacy for the future.

When You "Lose It"

There will be times—many, many times—when it feels like nothing works, and you just can't stop yourself from losing your temper. Kids can drive even the most rational and patient parent into a frenzy. It happens to everyone and it's not the end of the world. If you lose it, the key is to make up and move on. It doesn't diminish your authority to apologize for being human.

Helen, the divorced mother of four, including eleven-year-old twin boys, a ten-year-old girl, and a five-year-old girl, was one of the most unflappable moms I'd ever met—especially considering that she, as a single parent, was handling everything on her own. She seemed a model of calm. I had the impression that a curse word had never darkened her lips. What finally sent her over the edge was her children's fighting.

"I had taken the kids to a local diner for dinner," she recalled. "It was a rare treat and we were all feeling good. But during the course of the meal, one of the twins, Pete, whispered something to his sister about a girl his brother James liked. She started giggling, then blurted out the name of the girl. James went ballistic and kicked her under the table—hard. She yowled, and I lost it. We don't allow hitting or kicking in our family. It's a primary rule. And there we were having a lovely dinner out in public, and I was furious with James for spoiling it. I lashed out at him and said some unbelievably harsh thing like 'You don't even belong in this family!' James burst into tears and I felt just terrible. I couldn't believe I'd said that. I immediately got up and hugged James. I told him, 'I'm terribly sorry for those words. I'm not proud of myself. I hope when you're ready you'll forgive me, but I know you can't right now.' He calmed down and we went on with our meal. As we left the restaurant, he whispered, 'I forgive you, Mom.'"

Helen learned that being able to apologize to your child after having said something truly hurtful can create a bond. Often, after an apology, you and your children feel closely connected. It's also a good time, when you're both calm, to discuss and review what happened and find ways to avert a "next time."

And while it's good to help children work out their own battles, sometimes your best response is simple empathy. When a child runs to you crying about some terrible injustice inflicted by a sibling, you might have a conversation like the one Marcella had with her daughter Anita:

ANITA:	She socked me in the back and I wasn't doing anything!
MARCELLA:	I bet you'd like me to go yell at her.
ANITA:	Yeah!
MARCELLA:	And you'd like me to punish her severely.
ANITA:	Yeah!
MARCELLA:	I know. She really makes you mad. Sometimes it's not easy to have a younger sister.

It would be unrealistic to think that a disgruntled child would always accept such a confirmation of feelings with equanimity and then bounce off happily to play. However, we don't have to (nor can we) magically make their upset feelings disappear. Only time can do that. Sometimes it's enough to help kids feel that they're being heard and taken seriously, even though we can't fix the pain or make their anger magically vanish.

That was Sharon's experience, as she described it in this surprising recollection of the day her three-year-old son told her he hated his eight-year-old sister:

"It bothered me when he said 'hate.' It's such an ugly word. I wanted to say, 'No, you don't really hate her.' Instead, I asked him why, not expecting him to give a reason. He surprised me with an answer: 'I hate Claire because you love her.' About all I could say was, 'Wow! What a feeling.' I gave him a hug and told him how much I loved him. That was all I said, but he gave me a big grin and hugged me back."

The Brighter Side of Rivalry

I once asked a group of parents who were upset about their kids fighting to imagine this scene: "Let's say you could wave a magic wand and all the fighting, rivalry, and competition stopped. When you asked your son to share a toy with his little brother, he would say, 'Sure, Mom. And if he breaks it, that's okay.' When you went out in the car, your daughter insisted that her brother sit in the front seat every time. When it came time to choose a TV program, your son said, 'Why don't we watch whatever Jenny wants to watch.' When the potato chip bag was almost empty, your daughter handed it to her brother and said, 'Here, you take the rest of the potato chips.'" By this point, all the parents were laughing at the absurdity of it, and a few were making faces. "Even if it were possible, I'm not sure I like the idea," ventured one mother. "Don't quote me on this, but, well, it sounds creepy."

These parents understood instinctively that something essential would be missing if their children never fought or competed or engaged in rivalry. One reason is that rivalry has a positive place in the lives of children. Simply put, it provides a way, in the safety of their own home, for them to test their limits, assert themselves, and learn to negotiate for what they want and need. It also brings them closer.

The bonds of loyalty between children don't always look the way we think they should. Parents who worry that their warring children are expressing their ugly sides need to look again. A man wrote to me about this experience: "When I was in the third grade, I was walking home from school one day when I happened upon a big boy bullying a small girl in the sandbox. She was crying. Feeling very brave and extremely mature for all of my eight years, I walked over to the two and verbally accosted the older boy, saying, 'Hey, stop beating her up.' The big boy looked up and responded, 'She's my sister!' 'Yeah,' chimed in the little girl, 'leave him alone. He's my brother and he can beat me up if he wants to!'"

Linda, the mother of two daughters, ages seven and nine, reported being surprised and impressed on an occasion when she expected rivalry and it didn't occur. "I recently lost sleep during the pee-wee cheering tryouts when it was obvious to me that Jill, the seven-year-old, would be picked for the squad and Anne, the nine-year-old, would not. On the day of the tryouts, my older daughter, Anne, handled herself very well and even asked Jill to help her practice gymnastics so she could do better next year. Jill, as excited as she was, managed to think of her sister's feelings, and she didn't gloat openly. She waited until Anne was out of the room to call her grandmother with the news. I assumed Jill would be bragging all over the place, but I was wrong. She wanted to make the disappointment less painful for Anne. I made sure to let Jill know how touched I was by her sensitivity toward her sister."

Most often, parents view warring siblings as a frightening portent of the future. One mother said woefully, "It terrifies me that my children won't be close when they grow up." But I have found that it helps to draw perspective from one's own memories. As one woman recalled in the mellow objectivity of time, "I know my parents hated it, but my brother and I truly enjoyed arguing when we were kids."

A young man, the father of two, remarked on how irritating and embarrassing his younger brother was when they were growing up—always horning in on his friends, never giving him a moment's peace, acting like a nerd. But it's different now that they're adults. "Things that annoyed me then do not bother me now," he said. "As I matured, I began to realize that my younger brother's conflicts with me arose from my not understanding his need to compete with me for attention and affection, and my need to compete with him. But now we share so much, especially the role of being parents ourselves, and the joint responsibility for our elderly mother. We even share fond memories of some of our worst fights."

I have an exercise that I often use with parents in which I ask them to list some of the things they'd like their children to feel toward one another. The list is always warm and fuzzy: love, trust, companionship, loyalty, allegiance, intimacy, affection.

Then I ask the parents to describe how they felt about their own siblings when they were growing up. The list is quite different: disgust, irritation, boredom, fury, embarrassment, hate, wishing they'd never been born, envy, resentment. (Occasionally, someone will throw out a few positives—protectiveness, admiration, love—but it's usually when they were fairly far apart in age.)

"What do you notice?" I ask them.

And, of course, it's perfectly clear. Their expectations for their own children are the complete opposite of the reality they experienced. "One more question," I say. "How do you and your siblings get along today?" This elicits mixed reviews, but most often people conclude that their childhood intolerance has mellowed, if not disappeared, with age.

The bond among siblings is absolutely unique. No other relationship involves the same intensity of closeness—both for better and for worse. As Linda Sunshine observed in her funny and poignant book, *"Mom Loves Me Best" (and Other Lies You Told Your Sister)*, "While you can hide your true self from Mom and Dad, your sister knows the core of you. She sees you being mean to the family dog; she hears you lying to your best friend; she knows when you've cheated on your chemistry paper. More than Santa Claus, your sister knows when you've been bad or good." While this depth of knowledge can lead to bitter assessments, there is something quite wonderful about it, too.

Chapter 5

Caught in the Fairness Trap

In the beginning, we orbit our parents like planets vying for the position closest to the sun.

—Laura M. Markowitz,
Networker magazine

Marsha, the mother of three, confessed to me, "I feel like a spinning top." The image made me smile. What a perfect description of the harried parent! I could almost visualize Marsha, a blur of activity as she raced to meet each child's demands. "These children are never satisfied," she sighed, "no matter how hard I try to make sure they all get their fair share. The problem is, what's a fair share when you have a ten-year-old, a four-year-old, and a two-year-old?"

Good question. And as Marsha discovered repeatedly, regardless of what she tried, one or the other of her kids was always left wanting more. And it really got maddening when all three of them were dissatisfied with her efforts. Many are the parents who tell me, "I feel like I can never win. They never appreciate how hard I try to be fair. They only notice when they think I'm not fair."

Children come equipped with highly sensitive antennae that detect even the smallest hint of inequity. You might say, they're born with a fairness gene. Long before they ever learn in American history classes that "all men are created equal," they are clamoring for justice and equality in every arena of life. Like bloodhounds zeroing in on the scent, they'll cry, "It's not fair!" Or, "He got more than me." Or, "Why do *I* have to when *she* doesn't?" Or, "You're always taking *his* side." Or, "How come he always gets to go first?" Or the most painful: "You love her better."

How easily parents are swept into this child-imposed guilt trip! They explain, justify, and rationalize. They go to superhuman lengths to measure out perfectly equal amounts of everything, from affection to the number of sprinkles on an ice cream cone. I know a mother who kept a chart on the refrigerator door noting which child was the last to ride in the favored front seat of the car. She thought she had successfully handled a recurring source of conflict until the day Jonas, her eldest, accused her of mistakenly writing down the wrong name:

JONAS: I didn't sit in the front seat yesterday. It was Carol. You made a mistake.

MOM: No, I didn't. I marked it down as soon as we came in the house.

JONAS: (ignoring what she said) That's not true. It's not fair. You're never fair.

As this example demonstrates, even parents who have programmed themselves to be fair soon learn the utter futility of their efforts. Life just can't be perfectly equal in every instance, and even when parents think they're being fair, children will unearth a discrepancy. Life becomes an exhausting march through quicksand.

One parent explained her position this way: "I tell my children, 'Fair is not equal.' " This rallying cry has been picked up by many parents in my workshops, and it pretty much states the truth of it all. Even so, kids are slow to get the message. They measure food portions, keep track of gifts, and possess faultless memories for trivia—from who chose yesterday's TV program to whose turn it is to push the grocery cart. Their eagle eyes are always scanning the situation. They tally up petty accounts to the point where it can drive you to distraction. You probably wonder why they have to do this, since you try so hard to be fair. Probably because often the issue isn't really about food or toys or TV or going first. It's about wanting your undivided attention and affection, and resenting having to share it.

The other reason kids make such a big deal about fairness is that it works. That is, they frequently succeed in getting a rise out of you. I have found that complaints of being unfair are far less common in households where parents manage to act indifferent to the accusations. One parent told me, "My usual answer when my kids say it's not fair is 'You're right.' That seems to defuse their complaints." By contrast, the parent who responds by trying to justify or "fix" the unfairness gets caught in the trap.

Trying to be fair—and failing—is one of the most aggravating aspects of bringing up siblings. Sandra, a parent in one of my workshops, provided this dialogue between herself and her son Myles, which several other parents agreed sounded boringly familiar to their homes.

MYLES: Josie always gets everything.
SANDRA: Oh, Myles, that's not true.
MYLES: Yes it is! You gave her the last bowl of Cocoa Crispies, even though I wanted them, too.
SANDRA: Josie asked first.
MYLES: See! That's what I mean. She always gets everything.

When a child complains, "It's not fair!" it may be her way of expressing the wish to be loved solely and exclusively. That's impossible, of course. When you have two or more children, you can no longer grant the desire of any of them to be the one and only. But you can listen and respond to the deeper cry, which is: "Do you hear me? Do you see me as an individual? Am I separate, special, respected, interesting, enjoyable, lovable? Do you appreciate me for who I am?" Then, instead of counting the marshmallows in the hot chocolate, you can try to respond to the message behind the words.

Here are some suggestions you might find helpful.

Respond to Need, Not Sameness

The futility of struggling to achieve absolute equality is obvious. You would need superhuman powers and a flawless memory to pull it off. You would need the wisdom of Solomon, as well—and, frankly, given the choice, most kids would probably opt for splitting the baby in half. And even if you could, by some force of magic, give each of your children exactly the same amount of everything, it's not necessarily what they really want.

My own experience with my father taught me the truth of this. My father always had a hard time showing his feelings, and while I was growing up I never felt as if he really knew me or appreciated me as I was. He probably *did* care, but was unable to express it.

One day, when I was an adult in my thirties with children of my own, I finally got up enough nerve to ask my father, "Dad, do you really love me?" He was caught off guard by the question, and seemed embarrassed. He stumbled for a few seconds, then finally said, "Of course, I love all of my children the same."

He probably meant to be reassuring, but that was not what I wanted to hear. I was hurt that he was unable to come up with something special that he loved about me alone, rather than lumping me into a "same" category with my siblings. This experience reinforced my belief that when parents define equality as sameness, it doesn't make a child feel valued and unique. The line "fair is not equal" really means that you try to give each child what you can according to his or her need. Sometimes, that means treating one of your children with extra consideration.

Sara, the mother of ten-year-old twin boys, described an occasion when the need for special treatment outweighed her efforts to be fair. "I am very sensitive to being fair—perhaps too much so," she said. "But when you are dealing with twins, you feel compelled to make sure they both feel equally loved. One day last week when the boys came home from school, Ben seemed upset about something. He wasn't his usual chipper self. I knew something was wrong, but he shrugged off my questions until just before it was time for bed. Then he started crying and telling me about a kid at school who was mean to him, punching him on the arm and throwing his book bag on the ground. I wanted to give him a chance to talk, so I said, 'Let's go downstairs and get a warm drink.' His brother, Eric, jumped in with lightning speed, saying, 'Mom, it's three minutes until nine. How come you're letting Ben go downstairs with you?' I felt a bit guilty for giving Ben this privilege, but I knew he needed it and Eric didn't. I told Eric as nicely as I could, 'Ben needs me right now. Sometimes it's necessary to bend the rules.' He didn't really appreciate my point at that moment. He was too busy keeping score. But I think the message will make more sense to him when it's his turn to get extra attention."

Stepsiblings: The Ultimate Unfairness

The issue of fairness gets even more complicated when parents remarry and children from other marriages enter the picture.

Kids are already poised to accuse you of unfairness, and what could be more unfair in the eyes of a child than to introduce ready-made siblings into their universe? At least with birth siblings there's a natural growth period during which children learn to establish their place in the family. When parents remarry and bring someone else's children into the house, it can seem like the ultimate insult.

The appealing images of big, happy combined households are rarely borne out. More typically, children are intent on protecting their territories—including their stuff, their pets, their place at the table, their rooms, and the precious attention of their birth parent.

As one stepmother recalled, "It was so hard to love my fourteen-year-old stepson. He pushed my buttons every minute and never missed a chance to complain about how my daughter got preferential treatment, which was a complete distortion. I often found myself wishing he wasn't there. I was jealous of the time he took away from my three-year-old, not to mention how he manipulated his father to make me the bad guy. I felt he was turning our formerly happy home into a war zone."

New stepparents are normally quite agitated by their children's refusal to fall into line. "This is hard for all of us," sighed Frances, whose second marriage brought together her twelve-year-old daughter, Gail, with her new husband's five-year-old daughter, Simma. "Gail is old enough to understand that we're going through a transition. I really count on her cooperation, but I'm not getting it. It's infuriating when she claims Simma is getting too much attention. After all, Simma is five and Gail is a big girl of twelve. The other day she flew into a snit because I bought Simma a toy. It's not as if Gail doesn't get plenty of things herself. She should know better."

"I think Gail must be giving you a hard time right now because she's feeling left out—although I'm sure that's not your intention," I told Frances. "Have there been many changes since her stepsister moved in?"

"Well, you know, it's been hectic," Frances said. "Gail and I don't have as much time alone, but I can't very well ignore Simma's needs."

I suggested that Frances make an effort to plan a night out for just herself and Gail, even if she had to hire a baby-sitter. She agreed, and later reported this conversation they had over dinner in a favorite restaurant from the "old days."

GAIL: I miss us just being alone. Remember when we used to come here all the time?

FRANCES: I miss it, too, honey. I realize I haven't spent as much time with you lately.

GAIL: We're not the same family. You don't really care about me anymore.

FRANCES: Is that what you think?

GAIL: No . . . I guess not. But Simma's such a little brat. She interferes with everything.

FRANCES: Having a new sister in the house is hard.

GAIL: She's not my real sister.

FRANCES: Mmm-hmm . . .

GAIL: When she's around, which is always, I don't seem to matter.

FRANCES: (trying to inject humor) Hey, join the club! Simma is very demanding. Five-year-olds can be like that. Listen, can I tell you a secret?

GAIL: What?

FRANCES: Sometimes I too miss the way it used to be when it was just us. You're the only daughter who is all mine, and that makes you extra special. But I would hate for Simma to feel she's not welcome in our home. Maybe you could help me with that.

GAIL: Yeah, I guess so.

FRANCES: Great! I'd appreciate your ideas. I'm new at this stepfamily business, too.

This night out was a very important one for Frances and Gail. Frances's ability to listen to her daughter with empathy reminded Gail that she still had an important ally. "We decided that once a week we would go out together, just the two of us," Frances said. "Gail was very pleased with the idea, and frankly, I felt good about it, too. I hadn't realized how much I also had missed our former closeness. Even though Simma is now an important part of our lives, I don't want to jeopardize my relationship with Gail. I think that if Gail feels more secure that I'm still there for her, she'll reach a point where she doesn't resent Simma quite as much."

You can't expect your children to respond to a new family arrangement with instant enthusiasm and cooperation. Even adults have trouble doing that! But try, like Frances did, to keep the lines of communication open. Engage the whole family in a frank conversation about establishing new boundaries, rituals, and rules—maybe at regular family meetings. Remember that even small concessions, like an off-limits room, a special night out, or colored bins to separate possessions, can make a big difference in helping kids to feel respected and appreciated in their home.

Finally, be aware that stepchildren have the ability to wound you with the truth, so try not to take it personally. Monica, the stepmother of a ten-year-old boy, Bobby, managed to stick to the issue at hand and not lose her cool when he complained about the house rules being unfair:

BOBBY: You're not my mother. You can't tell me what to do.

MONICA: Number one is certainly true. You're right, I'm *not* your mother. But number two is a horse of a different color. Your father and I have agreed on certain rules which we expect you to follow.

Monica admitted that she found it difficult not to lash back in anger when Bobby got defiant and pulled the "you're not my mother" routine. But it was much more effective to separate the two issues. "Besides," Monica said, "by agreeing with him that I wasn't his mother, which was the truth, I took away his most powerful weapon."

How to Avoid the Fairness Trap

Parents often ask, "How can I be fair?" That's the wrong question. As we've demonstrated, to achieve fairness (or the perception of fairness) is impossible in every instance. What parents need are tips for handling fairness complaints when they arise. Sometimes simple things work best. Here are some of my favorite techniques.

❧ *Don't keep saying "life is unfair."*

Parents often tell me that when they get pushed up against the wall, they can't think of anything else to say but "life is unfair." (Judging by the responses to my questionnaire, it may be one of the most frequently repeated statements in American households!) Of course, it's completely ineffective. Children cannot grasp the broad, philosophical fact of life's unfairness. They can notice only that their brother's toy is more appealing or that their sister's juice glass is filled higher. When you respond to an accusation of unfairness with the statement that life is unfair, you are denying your children's very real feelings. You're also ignoring the fact that in a child's mind, "life is unfair" really means "*Mom* is unfair." That's what Kyle's mother discovered:

KYLE: It's not fair that Greg gets to go to camp and I don't. He gets everything.

MOM: Greg is older. You can go to camp too when you're ten.

KYLE: I want to go to camp this year. It's not fair.

MOM: Life's not fair.

KYLE: *You're* the one who's not fair!

Consider the difference had Kyle's mother simply said, "I know." She would have affirmed Kyle's feelings and probably stopped him from continuing his complaint. It's hard to make a counteraccusation when a parent says, "I know." Instead of contradicting him, Kyle's mother would have acknowledged his feelings. She might also have responded in this way:

KYLE: I want to go to camp this year. It's not fair.

MOM: You wish you were old enough to go to camp this year. It's so hard to wait!

This response would not have made Kyle feel less disappointed. But he might have felt somewhat comforted. It can be hard to be the younger child having to watch older siblings get to do things first. On some level, the younger one probably understands that his time will come. Still, it makes a big difference if you try to understand the frustration instead of trying to talk a child out of his wishes. One mother told me that she was able to express empathy when her three-year-old daughter cried on the day her six-year-old brother started first grade. She said, "I remember like it was yesterday being four years old and sitting forlornly on the window ledge watching my brothers go off to school. I wanted so desperately to be with them, to be old enough to have my own lunch box and book bag. Some days I sat by the window for hours waiting for them to come home. So I know how my daughter feels, and I tell her about when I was a little girl who wanted the same things so badly."

🐱 *Respond to the desire, not the complaint.*

I was struck by the sheer simplicity of one mother's approach, as described by the late parenting expert, Dr. Haim Ginott. She had just dished out plates of scrambled eggs, which to her looked like two exactly equal portions. One of her children inspected the other's share and cried, "You gave her more!" Without missing a beat, this mother replied, "Oh, so you'd like more eggs." She avoided the trap, squelched the brewing fight over eggs, and gave her child a moment of attention. It was a very apt response.

There is usually an unspoken request underlying a child's complaint of unfairness. You can help your children by keeping the issues straight yourself—as this mother did in the following dialogue:

MICHAEL: I saw that! You gave Molly another cookie.

MOM: Do you want another cookie, Michael?

MICHAEL: You love her more.

MOM: Gee! I thought we were talking about cookies, not love.

Many parents can't resist the stabbing guilt that accompanies a child's accusation that they favor another child in the family. Our instinct is to rush to prove otherwise, which is exactly what the child has in mind. Which brings me to the next point.

🐱 *Recognize the way kids program you to react.*

Parents often get defensive when their children accuse them of being unfair—especially when they bend over backward trying to be evenhanded. One mother turned the tables on her kids during an arduous "count the cookies" routine. "They were asking me, as they often do, to keep score so everything would be divvied up equally," she said. "I told them flippantly, 'Well, okay, if you want me to be the scorekeeper, remind me the next time I punish one of you to be sure to punish the other.'" Her kids actually laughed. "For a rare moment, they saw I couldn't be conned," she said proudly.

Wise parents give according to need, even when their children can't see the wisdom of it. You needn't apologize for recognizing that not everyone needs the same attention all the time. As writer Phyllis Theroux put it, "Rearing three children is like growing a cactus, a gardenia plant, and a tub full of impatiens. Each needs varying amounts of water, sunlight, and pruning."

When Sue was at the mall, she bought her nine-year-old daughter a much-needed pair of shorts, creating a storm of protest from seven-year-old Marta:

MARTA: Why didn't *I* get any shorts?

SUE: I bought shorts for your sister because she needed them. Are you mad because I didn't bring you anything?

MARTA: Yeah, I'm mad.

SUE: Do you remember two weeks ago, you needed blue jeans and we went to the mall and bought them?

MARTA: Okay, okay, I get it!

Sue admitted that she was tempted to launch into a long lecture in order to justify her purchase. She also briefly considered bribery—"We'll buy you shorts next week." Instead, she made her point in a more convincing way. Marta got it and went off to play, not mentioning the shorts again.

❧ *Give your kids permission to disagree.*

It's normal to wish that your kids will agree with your decisions and be perfectly understanding. That's why so many parents get tangled in futile justifications and explanations. They hope that their kids will "see the light." It's a hopeless goal! Kids want what they want; they're simply not going to say, "Okay, Mom, you're right. Leroy is feeling sad so he should get to pick the movie." Or, "It's only fair that Marcella should be allowed to stay up until nine o'clock. She's ten years old." Or, "Thank you, Mommy, for reminding me that it's my turn to do dishes. I really appreciate the way you keep track of things."

I'm sure you see how unlikely any of these scenarios are. Since you can't expect applause and gratitude when you set limits, you must make decisions based on your own good judgment, whether or not your children like it. Give up the need to have your children agree with you. Don't let them be the final arbiters of what's fair. A father who understood this shared a conversation he had with his thirteen-year-old daughter, Brenda.

BRENDA: I can't believe you let Jack go to the mall with his friends, but you won't let me go. What makes him so special?

DAD: Jack is fifteen and I feel safer letting him go.

BRENDA: That's so unfair! You're discriminating against me!

DAD: I know you disagree and are disappointed, but when it comes to safety, the issue is not negotiable. I'm not comfortable letting a thirteen-year-old girl go alone to the mall.

This father didn't respond by trying to explain the reasoning behind his decision, criticizing his daughter for not seeing his point of view, or just getting angry and exploding. He acknowledged his daughter's right to disagree without changing his position.

❧ *Enlist your kids to help make things fair.*

Why should the entire burden be on you, the harried parent? Tell your kids you want them to help figure out solutions. For example, if they're always bickering about which after-school TV program to watch at four-thirty, tell them, "You guys sit down and figure out how you're going to solve this problem so you don't fight about the TV every day." Give them suggestions for problem solving, then leave the room. When Eric and Todd were young, I got so fed up with the daily battles over whose turn it was to do the dishes that I finally declared they would have to work it out between themselves. "Look, you guys," I said, "I am tired of hearing this discussion every day. I want you to go sit down and figure out how you're going to get the dishes done. Period." They disappeared into their room, and I could hear the sounds of elaborate negotiations, trading of toys, the drawing up of complex contracts. Eventually they emerged. Todd went into the kitchen to do the dishes. Eric began to assemble the items he'd promised to give his brother in exchange for getting out of dish duty. Both boys were satisfied with the outcome, because Todd didn't really mind doing dishes, while Eric would gladly give up his most prized possessions to avoid doing that job. I was pleased that the boys had worked it out on their own without my intervention. Whether or not *I* thought it was fair was less important than their arriving at a mutually acceptable solution.

❧ *Tickle their funny bones.*

Often, the best way to handle a fairness complaint is to use humor. Humor can work wonders, even with the most disgruntled child. For example, one of my workshop parents told us how she responded when her daughter complained that she favored her sister: "You're wrong. I feel exactly the same way about both of you. You both drive me crazy!" Another parent joked to her grumbling teenage son, "Boy, we'd better solve this now so you won't have to spend thousands of dollars on psychiatrist bills when you're grown up."

I also enjoyed the solution of a mother whose four- and six-year-old went to maddening lengths to compare amounts of juice in their glasses. A typical scenario went something like this:

AMY, six: Joel got more than me.
JOEL, four: I did not. I'm just sipping and you're gulping.

AMY: I am not gulping.

JOEL: I saw you, I saw you!

AMY: Mommeee!

She purchased two plastic glasses with measurement scales on the side and made a big production of pouring out exactly the same amount of juice every time. "I was trying to make a dramatic point," she explained. "And it worked." Eventually, the children grew impatient with the process, and this dialogue with Amy followed:

AMY: I don't want to use that glass. I want my Little Mermaid glass.

MOM: It doesn't have a measurement on it.

AMY: I don't care!

MOM: But what if Joel accidentally gets more than you?

AMY: Mom! I said I don't care.

• *Remember that "equality" isn't always best.*

The prominent parenting educator Eda Le Shan has written that trying to be fair results in less caring—exactly the opposite of what you intend. She illustrates her point with the story of a teacher: "A young teacher described her experience in teaching a class of twenty children. During the first year she wanted to be fair and show no favoritism. She decided never to do anything for one child if she could not do it for all of them. At the end of the year she reported that she felt she didn't have a warm, close relationship with any child in the class. The fact was, of course, that all she had ever given any child was one twentieth of herself, and that was never enough. The next year she relaxed. When a child needed her attention, he got it, even to the exclusion of others. Each child got the attention that suited his own needs and interests. At the end of the year each child had had one hundred percent of his teacher at one time or another, and she had made twenty enthusiastic friends."

I like this story because it debunks the notion that giving the same means giving your best.

Sometimes parents really get stuck when they set fairness precedents that they're uncomfortable with but don't know how to stop. Kelly, a mother in my workshop, described how her good intentions backfired. "James, my oldest, was a very needy child, and when Teddy came along, I wanted to make sure James didn't feel displaced. On Teddy's first birthday, we had a big family party, and I bought a gift for James so he wouldn't feel left out. Well, that started this whole thing for years where James would say, 'Teddy's birthday is coming up. What are you getting *me*?' I cringe every time, but I don't know how to extricate myself from the tradition."

I encouraged Kelly to go ahead and end the tradition, but give her kids fair notice. "Since James is the child who might really balk, why not make the change on his birthday, announcing, 'This is your day, not Teddy's. We'll get Teddy a present on his birthday.' "

Every child loves to have his or her moment in the sun. But they can learn to enjoy watching others have their moments, too.

👋 Relinquish fairness as a goal.

Who needs the extra pressure of keeping track of which child took the first bath yesterday, or who was the first one to get a kiss when you came in the door from work, or who picked the bedtime story two weeks ago? When a child complains about not getting equal treatment, don't argue. Just try to address what you think he really needs at that moment —an extra hug, a moment of undivided attention, an acknowledgment that he is annoyed or frustrated, or a compliment. You'll find that he cares less about equality than about getting your undivided attention for a moment. Paula discovered this when her five-year-old, Robert, engaged her in this conversation:

ROBERT: Everything is always Joni, Joni, Joni around here.
PAULA: Joni's only two.

ROBERT: You play with her in the bathtub every night. You
          don't play with me.

PAULA: (surprised because Robert made a big deal about tak-
          ing baths alone) I'd love to play with you in the bath-
          tub!

ROBERT: You would?

PAULA: Oh, yes. It was always my favorite thing to do. I was
          so disappointed when you decided you were old
          enough to take baths alone.

ROBERT: Well, at least you still have Joni to play with.

PAULA: Yeah, but it's not the same.

ROBERT: Don't worry, maybe we could play in my fort instead. I
          think you might like that.

PAULA: Okay! Take your bath and put on your PJs and we'll
          have storytime in the fort.

Robert was delighted and he ran off to comply. He didn't want Paula
to give him a bath or treat him like a baby. He just wanted to recapture
a feeling of nighttime nurturing that he was missing since becoming the
big boy of the house.

Paula's response was a good example of a parent responding to
need, not trying to achieve sameness. An infant and a five-year-old
have different needs, as do a ten- and a fifteen-year-old. When you hear
your children ignoring this reality and clamoring for what they have
long since outgrown or have yet to grow into, try to listen to what they're
really asking for behind the words.

Chapter 6

"I Can't Believe How Different They Are!"

When they were young, Eric and Todd seemed as different as night from day. Eric, my first child, was cautious and approached new situations anxiously. Todd would jump into new experiences impulsively, rarely anticipating or worrying about the consequences. I used to marvel that two children born of the same parents could be so very different. I had expected them to resemble one another. How easily I had forgotten how unalike my own brother and I were! In reality, parents can expect that their children will be more different than similar and prepare for it. In all the years I've worked with parents, I've almost never heard one exclaim, "My children are so alike!" The one exception is identical twins, and even they can be strikingly dissimilar.

Parents often tell me that the arrival of their second child threw them for a loop. They were startled by the utter uniqueness of this new human being. Just when they thought they had a handle on the business of raising kids, this new and utterly original human being entered the picture to challenge their comfortable assumptions.

"All of my life I have wanted to be a mother," one of my students wrote. "Because I grew up as an only child, my wish was to be a mother to many children. I had all the typical daydreams . . . I would never scream or hit. And God forbid that I should ever say those terrible things my mother said to me: 'Because I said so!' 'Take that look off your face before I slap it off!' 'As long as you live in my house, you will follow my rules!'

"With my first child, I was able to stick pretty close to my parenting goals. But my second child has tested every and all limits, pushed every button, plucked my last nerve. I have screamed like all those other mothers that I vowed I would never sound like. By the time I took your class, I was on the verge of losing it."

We are ill prepared for the disparity between children—how one can be sunny and compliant while another can be aggressive and defiant. "My daughter makes me feel like a good mother, and my son makes me feel like a bad mother," said one woman. Her distress was clear, but so was her insight. The differences in our children's temperaments, talents, and capabilities are bound to elicit intense positive and negative feelings in us. These differences can give rise to uncomfortable tendencies to compare them and play favorites. And we're unprepared for the way we ourselves are different parents with each child. There's no such thing as a generic parent. Each child arrives at a distinct point in our lives. Each evokes a separate response in us— meshing or clashing with our own personality. A child may remind us, consciously or unconsciously, of a beloved (or not so beloved) family member, and that factor becomes part of the picture, whether we want it to or not. And pity the child who reminds you of the most annoying characteristics of a relative or ex-spouse! Although we can't help but feel these natural preferences and tendencies, it's important to be aware of them so we can avoid *acting* on them.

Does Birth Order Matter?

One morning in my workshop, Claudia, the mother of three, expressed worry that her oldest son, Brad, was becoming too bossy. She didn't like the way that Brad, at eleven, lorded it over his younger brother, age seven, and sister, four, acting like a little dictator. She complained that he related to them more like an imperious adult than a sibling. "Brad views himself as the enforcer of house rules," she said, "and he watches the other kids like a hawk to make sure they're obeying each and every rule. He's eager to take them on for every transgression. Of course, they resent it and plot against him."

Maureen, the parent of four children, said, "I have the same problem with Eileen—she's thirteen. I think it's an oldest child thing. I was the oldest of six, and I remember how I always played the junior mom, especially when our mother was around. I think I was trying to get on her good side by acting like the responsible one."

"I agree," laughed Sarah. "Maybe it's the firstborn gene." She went on to talk about a book she had just read about birth order. "Some child-rearing experts say that children tend to behave in certain ways depending on where they come in the lineup," Sarah said. "It makes sense to me."

Some of the parents in my workshops are very well read about parenting issues. And many of them are quick to label their children's behaviors as typical of one syndrome or another. The birth order discussion is one that comes up frequently, and I've noticed that parents tend to assign roles to each of their children—the bossy firstborn, the oft-neglected "sandwiched" middle child, the permanently "babied" last born, and so on. Anecdotal evidence alone suggests that there's some validity to the birth order equation, but I've always been bothered about placing such rigid labels on children according to their place in the family. In addition to birth order, there are many other factors that determine a child's temperament, personality, style, and role in the family. It seems to me that saying that all firstborns are leaders is the kind of stereotyping that is no more useful than claiming all only children are spoiled.

I am uncomfortable with absolutes and wary of generalities because it has been my experience that as soon as we think we've figured children out, they surprise us. As I look at my own children, the only reality I've observed is that their roles have kept changing. The minute I began to think one of them was a certain way, he showed me it wasn't necessarily the case. If we make birth order a rule, I suspect we will soon become flooded with exceptions—the shy, retiring firstborn and the bossy middle child; the tough, independent "baby" and the older child who prefers to sit on the sidelines; the only child who devotes her life to helping others, and the sister of four who never learns to share.

I shared my conflict about this subject with Zel Hopson, a counselor at the Nanaimo Family Life Association in British Columbia. Zel runs workshops for parents on the subject of birth order, and she reassured me that her intention was not to reinforce rigid labels. "Birth order is not so significant in and of itself," Zel told me. "But it is one of many clues toward understanding your children—and yourself, too. I say, why not consider it a tool that may increase our insight and understanding?"

Zel has learned her most valuable lessons by observing parents. In her workshops on birth order, she noticed that those who were the eldest in their own families tended to dominate conversations and wanted to be in charge. Those who were middle children tended to be more casual and comfortable, not that concerned about the outcome. And those who were the youngest seemed to be the least task oriented, preferring to let others take the lead. Zel is familiar with all of these tendencies, having seen them played out many times. But she is careful to acknowledge that tendencies are only that; they are not hard and fast truths. Her message is, use birth order guidelines if they're going to be helpful, but don't use them to oversimplify and stereotype your child's personality or behavior.

In his article, *Places Everyone* (Health, 1992), Stephen Harngan summed up my thoughts about birth order. He wrote: "The big problem with assessing birth order is the almost impossible task of getting a clear focus on what it is that's being studied . . . Take, as an example, a family with four siblings. The children might have been born one after another at regular intervals . . . But what if they came along in sets of two that were separated by a wide gap of years? . . . What if the firstborn was a boy, and all the rest were girls? . . . The permutations of gender, spacing, and circumstance are so endless and complicating that it hardly seems worthwhile trying to sort through them."

As I listened to the comments of parents on this subject, I realized how essential it is that parents be aware of the ways in which we can pigeonhole our children according to their birth order, thus creating preconceived expectations. Our language even reflects this. For example, the oldest child might be told, "You should know better." "Act your age." "Set an example." The second born is easily measured against the oldest, and can be made to feel diminished: "Your brother is bigger; he goes first." "Your sister is older; she knows better." And the youngest may be excused with "He's only a baby," or "She's still so young; we have to make allowances for her." Over time, these subtle images take hold and children begin to define themselves and their siblings as weak, strong, smart, clumsy, pretty, mature, or babyish, depending on their predetermined role in the family.

It's tempting to assign labels because it does simplify things. But it can also be limiting. And sometimes negative labels become self-fulfilling prophecies. This was Serena's experience.

"As the third of three, I always felt like the cover of a book rather than its contents," Serena said. "My sister, the oldest, and my brother, the only boy, were expected to be achievers. Nothing was expected of me except just getting by. As a result, I never felt particularly smart or clever, and I avoided the spotlight. I still do." It's impossible to know whether Serena's style is the result of nature or nurture, but the expectations of her parents—or the absence of expectations—clearly contributed to her lack of confidence in herself.

Alert parents look for ways to enhance each child's unique qualities, without resorting to labels. Here are examples of the difference between the two:

Labeling	*Encouraging*
"Carla's our little artist."	"Carla, what a colorful picture! I get such pleasure from your paintings."
"Don't mind Jeff. He's our shy one."	"I guess Jeff isn't in the mood to talk right now."
"John's our jock. He's the athlete in the family."	"John hit a home run and his team won the Little League championship. What a day that was!"
"Bonnie has never had a head for math."	"What can we do to help Bonnie with her math problems? She's having trouble with fractions."
"Elba is sweet, but she's such a scatterbrain. If her head weren't attached, she'd probably leave it at the mall."	"Elba needs practice in focusing on one thing at a time. We're helping her become less distracted by making lists, since she's very visual."

As these examples demonstrate, a label is defining and limiting, while a sensitive observation encourages children to see themselves as capable of making changes and finding solutions.

When we talk about birth order in my groups, parents sometimes express concern that their firstborns will be shortchanged by the arrival of a sibling. Once the sole object of parental love, attention, and resources, the number one child can no longer receive that intense focus. As one mother lamented, "I wish I had two laps, but I don't." I find this concern to be healthy, since awareness of the firstborn's feelings of displacement helps parents find ways of reassuring him and making him feel secure. As we discussed in Chapter Two and elsewhere, there are many practical techniques available to help firstborns feel less dethroned by number two.

What's more, I find that parents in my groups worry that their second borns will also be shortchanged, simply because they aren't able to give them as much. With two children, it's a fact that there's less time and fewer resources, and these grow skimpier still when there are three or more children. Parents are busier. Life is more frantic. It's not unusual for family videos, picture albums, and baby books to reflect this reality. Your firstborn's baby book may detail the minutiae of her existence, right down to the day and hour she cut her first tooth, learned to roll over, and took her first bite of solid food. Your second child's book might contain hastily scrawled notations every few weeks or so, while your third child's book has little more than the date of birth and the baby's initial weight. This is not to mention the disparity in the number of pictures! Many second and third children are aware of this disparity and the significance is not lost on them. It's worth the extra effort to equalize the amount of pictures, home movies, and videos we collect.

Of course, parents feel awful when their children mention this inequity. They wonder if a second child risks feeling second best—as one parent put it, "A perpetual Avis to his brother's Hertz."

To help parents gain perspective during those times when they worry about what their number two and three and four children are experiencing, I sometimes ask parents themselves to write down the advantages and disadvantages of not being the firstborn. Their lists look something like this:

Disadvantages to Being Number Two or More:

- The excitement and anticipation don't compare to the first time around.
- Parents have less time.
- You never get to be an "only."
- Not as many photos in the album.
- Not as much footage on the VCR.

- Grandparents may make less of a fuss.
- People compare you to your older brothers or sisters.
- You're stuck with hand-me-downs.

Advantages to Being Number Two or More:

- Parents are more experienced and less uptight.
- There are older siblings to teach you the ropes.
- Your siblings are ready-made playmates.
- Parents are less "intense" and can roll with the punches.
- There is more activity and more fun.
- Sometimes an older sibling can act as a role model and inspire you to aim higher.

Making lists helps dispel the guilt as parents realize that although their later children miss some of the advantages of being first, there are special benefits that weren't available when they were getting their feet wet with number one.

I like the way the writer Anna Quindlen articulated it: "The first child got me shiny new like a new pair of shoes, but he got the blisters, too. The second child got me worn, yes, but comfortable."

Of course, all the birth order theories go out the window when you're dealing with twins, triplets, or other multiples. As they grow, these children find their own place in the family and develop their own style, unrelated to the order of their birth. I've noticed, however, that few parents of multiples are able to let things develop without a great deal of anxiety. Mostly, they're worried that their children won't feel like unique individuals, and they bend over backwards to make sure each child is singled out. While in itself that's not a bad goal, multiples also need the space to grow apart from their siblings, and the opportunity to find their own style and role. But that's easier said than done.

Mona, the mother of identical twin boys, talked about the difficulty of encouraging each child's sense of uniqueness, against daunting odds. "Appearancewise, Michael and Foster are interchangeable," she said of her nine-year-old sons. "If you know them, it's easy to tell them apart because their personalities are quite distinctive. Michael is Mr. Sociability, and Foster is quieter. But most of the time, people don't make the effort to learn which is which. Their own grandmother, who sees them a couple times a month, still says, 'Oh, I can never tell you boys apart.' She doesn't help matters by buying them identical clothes on their birthdays. Their teacher makes them wear name tags because she can't bother to learn their identities. It gets them so mad that they sometimes switch tags just to get back at her. People expect them to be interested in the same things, and they're surprised when they're not. I could go on and on. No matter how hard my husband and I try to make each boy feel special, it's like the whole world is conspiring to keep them identical. I'm afraid they'll grow to resent each other. What can I do?"

There's no easy solution to Mona's dilemma, although from the sound of it, her sons don't resent each other as much as they resent other people's unwillingness to see their separate identities. I encouraged Mona to have a talk with the teacher to see if instead of name tags they could be identified with an item of clothing or a color. I suggested to Mona that she have the same conversation with the children's grandmother. "You can also be somewhat straightforward with Michael and Foster," I said. "Let them know that you, too, find it frustrating when people lump them together because you see them as such individuals. It's okay to prepare them for the inevitability that there will always be people who will try to treat them like clones. At the same time, constantly reinforce with them that you don't think that at all—and neither should they."

Today's parents have access to many resources about issues like birth order and multiples. Some of them are listed in Appendix A. Just be careful not to get so bogged down in theories that you lose sight of the practical point of it all—which is to admire each of your children as an original, not a dimmer copy of someone else.

Playing Favorites

"I have a guilty secret," Lynn confessed to my group one morning. Everyone perked up their ears since the telling of these so-called guilty secrets inevitably strikes a chord of recognition in other parents.

"I prefer my eight-year-old son, Peter, to his twelve-year-old sister, Candace," Lynn said shamefacedly. "Not just sometimes, but all the time. Peter is a living doll, a real sweetie. Candace is disobedient, sassy, crabby, and completely uncooperative—whether I ask her to dry the dishes or watch over her brother. She hates baby-sitting for Peter, even though I pay her. In fact, she hates Peter, period."

"Twelve is a tough age," a woman in the group murmured sympathetically.

Lynn shrugged. "It was just as bad when she was ten. She thinks Peter gets all the breaks and nothing I do convinces her otherwise. But most of the seeming 'breaks' Peter gets have to do with his being younger. He's only eight and he needs more care and attention than a preadolescent."

"Can you describe a typical situation?" I asked Lynn.

She rolled her eyes. "There are so many. Just this morning we were running late. It was complete chaos, the school bus was due in three minutes, and I asked Candace to help me pack Peter's lunch. She picked that moment to scream at me, 'I'm not your slave!' and went storming out. Peter missed the school bus, and I wanted to wring her neck."

"I can understand your frustration, Lynn," I said. "But can you step back for a minute and consider what Candace might be feeling? When a child constantly makes the point that you're being unfair, they're usually feeling unappreciated. They have a sensitive radar detector that picks up when we're annoyed or resentful. It's almost as if by their defiant behavior they are really saying, 'Can you love me even though I'm not easy?' Perhaps when Candace gets sassy or crabby, that's what's going on underneath."

The following week, Lynn returned to the group with this story. "I was on the phone and Candace came into the room and started talking to me."

LYNN: (waving her away) Stop interrupting me. Can't you see I'm on the phone?

CANDACE: (furious) I'm invisible around here!

Candace storms out of the room and when she finishes her phone call, Lynn finds her in her bedroom sulking.

LYNN: What's bothering you?

CANDACE: Never mind. I wanted to talk to you but you were too busy . . . as usual.

LYNN: You seem really angry at me.

CANDACE: When Peter needs something, you drop everything. But I'm like an orphan in this house.

Candace looked so miserable that Lynn felt a sudden rush of compassion. Suddenly, she realized that Candace's perception needed to be validated. Instead of trying to persuade her that she was wrong, Lynn tried to acknowledge her sadness and anger.

LYNN: Wow! That must be a crummy feeling!

CANDACE: (resentfully) You should only know.

LYNN: It sounds like you need some T.L.C. Why don't we drive to the mall?

CANDACE: (brightening) What? Just the two of us? Will we have time to look for some new sneakers?

Later, Lynn remarked on the incident. "Once I was able to feel compassion instead of irritation, it worked like magic. That really taught me a lesson. I started to see Candace in a more positive light and give her some space—not taking it so personally when she's moody. I'm also trying not to expect her to be cheerful like her brother, and that's helping."

Most parents find that every child has the capacity to drive them nuts at some point in his or her development. The contented baby might become the unmanageable toddler. The lovable young girl who always confided in you can become the recalcitrant, sullen teenager who can't stand to have you around. It's normal to find that one of your children is more difficult than another at any given time. It's also normal to prefer one child to another—usually the one who is giving you the least amount of trouble or the greatest amount of pleasure. "Jane is so sunny and dear," a mother in one of my workshops sighed. "And her brother is so oppositional. Sometimes I find myself thinking how much I prefer my daughter, and I hate it. How can I feel this way? How can a good mother say that she doesn't like to be with one of her children?"

I assured this mother that it was more normal to have a favorite than it was to love all one's children equally. I also reminded her that the child who is today's favorite might well be tomorrow's challenge. "There's nothing wrong with *feeling* this way," I said. "The danger is when we *act* on the feeling." Then, addressing the group, I asked, "Has anyone here ever found yourself having a conversation in your head about one of your children that went something like this: 'You are the most *trying* child . . . I wish you'd get laryngitis for a week . . . You're such a *pain* . . . I can't *stand* being with you . . . I wish you were more like your *brother.* . . .' "

The mothers in the group laughed loudly and somewhat guiltily. "Does it sound dreadful?" I asked. "How could any loving parent think such things?" Well, I believe every parent has such moments. Children can be so trying, especially when we're already under stress. If only you could give yourselves permission to think your thoughts and feel your feelings. Remember, thinking isn't the same as doing. You might feel a warm glow whenever your cheerful four-year-old runs to hug you, while getting a knot in your stomach every time you pass the big Keep Out! sign on your ten-year-old's bedroom door. But these are normal emotional responses. Sometimes it's just plain hard to respond in a loving way to a child who is constantly disruptive, or one who has trouble getting along with other children, or one who doesn't thrive socially or emotionally. Fortunately, as an adult you have the capacity to express more than the knee-jerk reactions. Not that it's easy. The ability to look beyond the overt behavior and respond with empathy to what you think a child needs requires an almost superhuman effort. But I'm constantly impressed by the strength and courage of parents who manage to do just that. And the results are often gratifying. Sometimes just a few days of pointing out what a child does right, or biting your tongue to avoid a familiar litany of criticisms, can make an enormous difference in transforming a child's provocative attitude.

It's also helpful to be aware that our preferences tend to shift, depending on children's ages and stages. Donna found this to be the case with her twelve-year-old son and ten-year-old daughter. "Until now, it has generally been easier to get along with Melissa," she reported in one of my workshops. "But as she hits preadolescence, she is definitely exhibiting more signs of teenage moodiness and mother disdain. Teddy, on the other hand, is easier and more reasonable than he's ever been—much less inclined to back himself into a corner from which no one can extricate him, least of all himself." Another mother said, "Thankfully, my favoritism is fleeting, and each child seems to have a special place in my heart on any given day."

Parents struggle daily with this issue, and sometimes hate to admit how strong their preferences can be at times. One week a group of mothers in one of my workshops explored some of their deeper concerns about feelings of favoritism.

"My eldest daughter and I get along better, partially because she is more mature, but also because she is more compliant and able to understand more of the reasons behind my actions," confessed Marcia. "I don't feel I favor either one when they act up together. But I am sometimes much stricter with my younger daughter and come down harder on her because she's so stubborn and argumentative." Marcia's point was interesting. It's understandable that a parent would tend to prefer the child who is more compliant. But there's sometimes an ambiguous message, as one father admitted about his fifteen-year-old son. "I want Jerry to be his own person, and not to feel he has to do whatever his friends are doing, but I get annoyed when he ignores *my* advice. I catch myself saying things that sound a lot like 'Be independent, but do it my way.'"

"Currently our eldest daughter, Marie, has been so aggravating—leaving her stuff all over, losing things, et cetera," Theresa said wearily. "She gets yelled at a lot, with no obvious change, of course. In contrast, our second daughter, Amy, is very responsible. We thought Amy had lost her gym uniform, but it turned up in her older sister's locker. It's almost impossible not to be constantly on Marie's case."

It's frustrating when a youngster is so forgetful and distracted, but it's unlikely that Theresa's anger at Marie will help her daughter be more careful about her possessions. It might only makes things worse, by calling attention to her shortcomings. Once a child gets the label of being irresponsible, she usually lives up to it, especially if the parents forget to notice and comment on the times she *is* thoughtful, considerate, and responsible.

Karen, who seemed to accept the fact that having preferences is okay, spoke up. "Each child appeals to some characteristic in each of us," she said. "Their styles are so different that sometimes if there's a particular interest, I allow myself to enjoy it with that child—like going to museums with my oldest son—and tell the others that I'll do something special that appeals to them another time."

"I felt a strong dislike for my older daughter Patricia for a few months," Grace confessed. "She was having problems with her schoolwork, and I was so worried that I didn't stop to think about why she was having trouble, especially since her younger sister, Erin, was doing so well. I felt—unfairly, I know—that she was deliberately trying to screw up, unlike her sister, who was such a serious, hardworking student. I even found myself siding with my younger daughter when they had disputes—simply because she was an easier child who was not causing me so much worry. I had to stop myself and consider what I was doing."

"Have you been able to see Patricia in a more positive light recently?" I asked.

Grace nodded. "Patricia's teacher called me in for a conference, and I was quite upset. I dreaded that all of my worst fears were being realized. But her teacher was supportive and insightful. She seems to really like Patricia, and she made a point of mentioning several of Patricia's strengths. And, she helped me to see things from Patricia's point of view. She said she thought my daughter had been deeply affected by her best friend moving away, and that's when her grades started suffering. I felt just terrible that I hadn't realized it. Later, I had a good talk with Patricia." Grace related their conversation:

GRACE: I saw Mrs. Phillips today. She really likes you, but she's been somewhat concerned about your school-work, and so have I.

PATRICIA: Why is everyone picking on me? I'm doing the best I can.

GRACE: I really believe you can do better.

PATRICIA: Yeah, that's because little Miss Perfect Erin can do no wrong.

GRACE: This isn't about Erin.

PATRICIA: So, what did she say?

GRACE: She thinks you feel bad because Sally moved away.

PATRICIA: Yeah?

GRACE: I'm so sorry your friend moved. That's such a bummer. I remember how you used to do homework together, and it must be hard not to have her here. Is there some way I can help you get through this?

PATRICIA: How can *you* do anything?

GRACE: Well, I'm not as much fun as Sally, but I can try to help you with your homework. And maybe this summer we can plan for you to visit Sally.

PATRICIA: Really?

GRACE: Yes. Friends are important. But you still have to get your lessons done.

PATRICIA: Okay! I can't wait to tell Erin!

"It was such a breakthrough for me," Grace told the group. "Patricia needed someone to understand her grief over losing her friend—someone to be her ally. Since our conversation, she's actually become more cooperative, and her grades have improved."

I was touched by Grace's story. It occurred to me how easily we parents get bent out of shape when our children do not fit our expectations. It's especially tricky when one child is going through a rough spell and the other acts like a candidate for sainthood. Then perspective becomes difficult. But as Grace found, avoiding judgments and looking beneath the surface can yield positive results.

Anna came to my workshop one day filled with worry about her oldest child, Rick, fourteen, a very challenging child. In addition to Rick, Anna has a daughter, Kara, twelve, and twin nine-year-old sons, Max and Adam. "The best way to describe Rick is that he never forgave us for having more children," Anna said grimly. "Every day, Rick makes it obvious how hostile he feels toward the other three."

As Anna talked about the dynamics among her children, searching for the source of Rick's anger, she began to see how her younger three had developed a kind of closeness that shut Rick out. "Kara is pleasant and well liked, and she has lots of friends," Anna said. "And when Max and Adam were born, well, they were twins, and everyone always pays a lot of attention to twins. Plus, Kara adored the twins and immediately became like a little mother to them. My younger three children have a wonderful relationship—but where does that leave Rick? Whenever we do anything as a family, Rick manages to create some kind of a scene. For example, everyone will want pizza and he'll make a fuss about wanting hamburgers. Or we'll go to the zoo, and he'll insist we see the giraffes first, even though we're heading for the monkey house. He always takes a contrary position, and when he doesn't get his way, he uses it as 'proof' that we prefer the other kids to him."

"Rick sounds very needy," I said. "Have you tried spending time alone with him?"

Anna nodded. "Yes, I've started to do just that on a more regular basis. For instance, last weekend I managed to take him out alone for breakfast. By himself, Rick is like a completely different child—sensitive, perceptive, and a pleasure to be around."

"He doesn't feel the need to compete," I observed. "I think your spending that time alone with him was really a gift. It gave you a chance to see another side of him."

It pained Anna that Rick felt like the least favored person in the family, maligned and misunderstood by everyone. Sometimes, in cases like this, where the resentments have solidified, it can take a huge effort to reverse the negative dynamics. A parent is not a magician; she can't force a child to feel loved when he feels so negative about himself. She can only do her best to let the child hear he is loved, encourage his cooperation within the family, and hope that in time he will come around. Most likely, for Rick, the solution will come from outside the family, when he finds an activity that engages his passion and makes him feel good about himself. Family counseling may help change the equation, as well, especially if the therapist or counselor can involve the siblings in a positive way, helping them work as a team rather than zeroing in on Rick as the spoiler, the problem child.

Unwittingly, some parents foster strife among their children by making comparisons or forcing them to compete. In spite of our best intentions, the urge is almost irresistible to say, "Oh, Joy started walking at eight months." Or, "Billy is a little slow. His sister was talking our ears off by this age." Or to them we might say, "It's funny, your brother never had any trouble with spelling." Or, "The one who brings home the best report card wins a prize."

Sandy, a woman in my workshop, said that she still remembered vividly how frustrated and resentful she felt as a child because of the competitive atmosphere in which she and her sisters were raised. "My father insisted that we continually compete with each other," she recalled. "Who could be the first into their pajamas, the first to brush teeth, the first to get dressed, the first to finish breakfast. It was unrelenting. I remember at dinner there was always a race to see who could drink her milk the fastest. There was a reward for the one who finished first, as long as she didn't snort it back up through her nose—then she got punished. I think our dad thought of these competitions as games, but it didn't feel that way—especially since Dad lavishly praised the winner and criticized the losers. One of his favorite expressions was 'You'll have to be quicker on the draw if you ever expect to get anywhere in this world!' Now, as I look back and try not to compare my own children, I wonder what made my father think that speed dressing or emptying a milk glass first was a virtue. All I know is that his method pitted me and my sisters against each other, instead of making us allies."

It is common for children to play "good kid/bad kid." When one is misbehaving, that's when you are most likely to see the angelic side of your other child. No child is all good or all bad, but when parents are having a particularly hard time seeing the good side in one of their children, I recommend that they create a "bug/brag" list. The bug/brag list, a method I have used for many years, is really quite powerful. You write down all of the things that bug you about your child. Then you turn the paper over and make a list of all the things you admire about your child. I have rarely met a parent who tried this exercise and did not feel better about a child—even the one who was pushing ten on the trouble meter. For example, the parent who lists "stubborn, messy, and selfish" on the bug list can begin to see the same child in a more positive light when she lists "affectionate, energetic, and creative" on the brag list.

"You Love Him More!"

Maureen, the parent of two, described how her efforts to make sure her toddler didn't feel left out in the early months following his brother's arrival backfired. "In the last five months since the baby was born, my husband and I thought it might work best if I took care of the baby most of the time and he took care of the two-year-old. Late one night while my husband was away, I was trying desperately to get the two-year-old to bed. He was being difficult, and as I tried to comfort him and take control of the situation, he blurted out, "Don't take care of me! Daddy takes care of me! You take care of Adam! Daddy loves me. You love Adam." I was stunned. I tried to explain to Alex that I loved him just as much as Adam, but actions speak louder than words. My husband and I changed our ways and we switched off, with my spending more time alone with Alex and my husband tending to Adam. Alex does seem to be less resentful of his baby brother."

Nothing pushes a parent's buttons more than the accusation that you love one child more than another.

MATTHEW: Who's your favorite, me or Daniel?

MOM: You're my favorite seven-year-old and Daniel is my favorite three-year-old.

MATTHEW: But who do you love the best?

MOM: You're the oldest, so I've loved you longer.

I thought this mother's response was very creative. However, parents need to realize that this is a question that has no single "right" answer. Of course, the worst answer would be "I love you best." You can be sure that the news will spread from one sibling to the other in a flash.

No one knows better than kids that talk is cheap—or can be—and sometimes the best way to handle a situation is with action.

KERI: You're always hugging and kissing the baby. You love him the most.

MOM: Don't be silly. I have plenty of love for both of you.

KERI: But you love him more. I can tell.

MOM: Keri, stop it. You're being ridiculous.

Later, this mother admitted that she became defensive instead of listening to her daughter's needs. She revised her approach the next time:

KERI: You're always hugging and kissing the baby. You love him the most.

MOM: Come here, sweetheart. You need a cuddle. Let me give you some extra hugs and kisses.

Darlene handled her son Damien's complaint of a perceived injustice with humor. "I wouldn't have tried this with Joseph, my younger son," she said. "But Damien has a good sense of the ridiculous, and a preposterous quip often works to get him out of a grumpy mood."

DAMIEN: I knew you loved him better!

DARLENE: (with mock horror) Oh, my! I'd been hoping to keep it from you, but now you know.

DAMIEN: (laughing) Oh, Mommy, don't be so silly.

Natalie told my workshop group that her two daughters constantly asked, "Who do you love the best?" And she always told them the same thing: "I love you both." But over time, Natalie learned to lighten up somewhat, and one day she had this conversation with her younger daughter, Suzanne:

SUZANNE: Who do you love the best, Chrissie or me?

NATALIE: You know the answer.

SUZANNE: Mom, Chrissie's not here. You can tell me who you love the best and she'll never know.

NATALIE: I'll bet you really want to hear that I love you more.

SUZANNE: Yes!

NATALIE: Even though you know that I love you and Chrissie just as much?

SUZANNE: Yes!

NATALIE: I guess you think if I say the words, it would be like magic. Hmmm . . . would you like me to say it even though you know how much I love both of you?

SUZANNE: (now giggling) Yes . . .

NATALIE: Okay, I love you more. There, I said it.

SUZANNE: (giving her mother a big hug) Oh, Mom, you're so wonderful. I know it's not true, but it's so much fun to hear you say it!

NATALIE: Oh, Suzy, you are a funny duck. And you give me such a lot of pleasure.

One of the mothers in the workshop expressed concern that Natalie might be treading on dangerous territory with her admission, even though it was made in jest.

"I thought about that," Natalie said. "It was one of those silly, spur-of-the-moment impulses. But I realized that Suzanne knew it was a game. I wasn't worried about her believing it. In a way, it cleared the air and became a joke—much better than my usual serious lecture."

When One Child Is "Special"

Helen's son, Joel, was overweight at thirteen, and she was the first to admit to me, "He's not a pretty sight." She was quite concerned that Joel's weight problem would make his teen years difficult. "I nagged him a lot about eating more nutritiously, and tried to get him to cut out junk food," Helen said, "but it didn't do any good. In fact, it probably made it worse, but I couldn't stop myself. It didn't help that his eleven-year-old brother was wiry and athletic. I'm sure this only made Joel feel worse." But one day Joel challenged his mother.

HELEN: Honey, why don't you have a piece of fruit instead of eating those potato chips. I think it would be better for your diet.

Joel didn't answer, and Helen repeated herself.

HELEN: How about an apple or a pear?
JOEL: (explosively) Mom! I know you hate me for looking fat. But why can't you ever just look at me on the inside, not the outside?

Joel stormed out of the room, as his mother gaped in horror. "I was struck dumb," Helen told me later. "I was very upset that Joel thought I hated him, and that I couldn't see beyond his weight problem."

Helen wanted to reassure Joel, but everything she considered saying sounded hollow and insincere. "I couldn't really say that weight didn't matter; he'd never believe me. I'd be a liar if I said his weight didn't bother me. But it helped to try seeing things from Joel's standpoint. I wanted to find a way to explain why it mattered—not because it made him unlovable, but because it made him unhappy and self-conscious around his peers." She finally had this conversation with Joel, choosing her words carefully.

HELEN: I was quite shocked to hear you say you thought I hated you. Do you really think that?

JOEL: Well, I know you hate me being fat.

HELEN: I apologize if I gave you that impression. I love you very much, Joel, and I also enjoy you. You can be so clever and funny, and I like that a lot. As for your weight, well, I wouldn't say I hate it, but it does worry me because I want you to be healthy and happy, and I know how hard it is when other kids make unkind remarks. It's my job to watch out for you, so of course I'm going to care.

JOEL: I guess . . . but do you have to nag?

HELEN: Yeah, I know my nagging is a pain, and not helpful. Maybe we can figure out a plan together, so it will be easier for you to decide what to eat and be more involved in planning the menus. I also know of a nutritionist who works with teens. Would you be willing to see her?

JOEL: That might be okay, but can it be a secret? I don't want *him* to tease me.

"Of course, 'him' referred to his loving brother," Helen said wryly. "I knew that part of my responsibility in supporting Joel was to make it clear to his brother that nasty cracks and fat jokes would not be tolerated."

Several months after the incident, Helen reported that Joel was still struggling with his weight, and she was struggling along with him. But their discussion had helped Helen to be more tolerant, and Joel became less defensive. It was an important turning point. "Even though he accused me out of anger, it took courage for Joel to say what he did," Helen said. "I've put a curb on my nagging, and he's been trying— although there have been lots of lapses. He actually liked seeing the nutritionist. I think it made him feel more adult. I also learned from her that it's not uncommon for young adolescent boys to have weight problems, which helped me get off his case a bit."

Helen was confronted with a struggle many parents face: what to do when one of your children has physical or emotional problems that set him apart from others in the family? There are two sides to the "special" child dilemma. The child, like Joel, might feel awkward and less lovable. On the other hand, a child who requires lots of extra attention because of a disability or a unique set of needs may cause the other children in the family to feel less valued.

Julia's nine-year-old son had a severe learning disability that required a special school and individual home tutoring. Julia was sensitive to the effect his additional demands might have on her two daughters, ten and five, particularly because as a child she herself had had a similar experience. "My younger brother was very sickly—he was a premature baby—and while I was growing up, I always heard 'Jack this and Jack that.' My mother hovered over him and monitored every sniffle. I was the healthy child, so my parents assumed I could take care of myself for the most part, and didn't need very much attention. I remember one morning, wanting to get some sympathy for myself, I told my mother I didn't feel well. If Jack had said that, Mother would have been all over him in a flash. But with me it was 'You don't look that sick.' Then she took my temperature and it was near normal, and off I went to school. Can you believe it, I actually envied Jack because he was sickly!"

Julia was determined that her daughters would not feel slighted in the same way. "I listen to their complaints very carefully and try to give them support when they're having a problem. Fortunately, they both love their brother, and we've tried to explain why he goes to a different school and needs extra tutoring. My oldest daughter is very good in school, and lately I've noticed her trying to help her brother with his homework."

Some parents have found that having children with special needs can build a tighter bond among siblings. Laura's eight-year-old daughter has become very protective of her four-year-old sister who has severe asthma, and she takes pride in knowing how to be helpful. "Rene is very watchful of Emmie's needs when they're out together," Laura said. "She is careful to warn people, 'Please don't put sesame seeds on my sister's bagel,' and she knows how to give Emmie her nebulizer. As a parent, I wish Emmie didn't have this illness, but when I see how Rene takes care of her sister, it makes me so proud. And Rene seems to feel really good about herself, as well."

Patricia, the mother of three, spoke very frankly about facing the difficult truth that her second child, Paul, had what the specialists labeled a "mild mental retardation." She reflected on what she had learned, and it was clear to the parents in the group that Patricia's experiences, painful as they were, had been quite a source of growth for her.

"When we first found out, we went into shock and numbness that lasted for some time. We made the rounds of clinical professionals. We were very worried about how Paul's disability would affect us all, especially his siblings. At first, it took a conscious effort to not treat Paul completely differently from his brother and sister, but with time we became more skilled. We learned how to allow Paul to do as much as he could for himself without rushing in too fast to help him. We tried to discipline them fairly, and to adjust our expectations of their different capabilities.

"We realized that as children they lived in two worlds—that of their own school friends and that of their exceptional family," she said. "Among their friends, they wanted to be considered 'part of the gang.' Yet being 'part of the gang' still demanded that they defend their brother. At times that has been difficult. They have been forced to mediate, to explain, and sometimes to choose between conflicting loyalties.

"If I were asked for suggestions on mothering an exceptional family,

I would offer the following: Look at the child first and the disability second, and encourage family and friends to do the same; try to spend an equal amount of time with each child, disabled or not; include the disabled child in all family activities; respond to siblings' questions about the disability factually and at an age-appropriate level; rejoice in and praise the efforts as well as the achievements of each child; enable your children to feel free to talk openly about the disability. Be sure every child's needs are met, but try to assure that your own emotional, mental, and physical needs are met as well. If you can, meet regularly with other parents of special needs kids who are struggling with similar challenges."

Enjoying the Uniqueness

Part of the excitement of having more than one child is discovering who each new individual will be, and seeing how the next child differs from the last. Real family life is a crazy quilt of multiple faces, styles, quirks, personalities, preferences, problems, and talents. Even though we sometimes wish it could be simpler—and bite our tongues so as not to say, "Why can't you be more like your brother?"—most parents agree that they wouldn't really want their children to be alike.

One mother who often admitted to feeling confused by the demands of her very different sons reflected about what it meant to have two children who were so dissimilar. "Both my husband and I find Martin, our older son, much easier to deal with," she concluded. "He has a gentle way about him and he's very reflective and affectionate. Stephen, in contrast, is a little bombshell, full of nonstop energy and noise. He's exhausting, but he has a very aggressive charm of his own. Also, the two have very different looks. Martin is a beautiful child, while Stephen is cute and perky looking but not especially beautiful. We always say jokingly that Martin has the beauty and Stephen has the charm. We enjoy watching their individual styles evolve, and notice how differently we respond to each of them. I'd be the first to admit that there are times I wish they were as alike as two peas in a pod. But, really, I can't imagine our family being any other way."

Memories of being noticed, listened to, and uniquely appreciated can last a lifetime. Forty-five years after the fact, Eve still remembered with great pleasure: "Two weeks before my eighth birthday, my sister was born. And my mom still had a birthday party for me with friends and a homemade cake! It was many years before I realized what an effort she had made to make me feel special, but it's something I've never forgotten. I remember the details of that birthday party as though it just happened—the games we played, the presents, my mother's face as she brought in the cake and watched me make a wish when I blew out the candles. I've probably thought about that day hundreds of times over the years. It made such an impression on me."

Another woman told me that she aspired to be as sensitive toward her children as her father was toward her and her sister. "I want each of my kids to have his or her moment in the sun," she said. "It's a concept my father taught me. I was very good at sports, and I was going to the state championship. And my father took me aside and said, 'Today is your day in the sun, and we're all going to be there for you. Another day will be your sister's day in the sun.' I hope I can do that for each of my kids."

Chapter 7

It's Okay to Be Angry

After a hectic day I finally sit down to dinner with my family for a little peace and quiet. . . . Suddenly my daughter will accidentally overturn a glass of ice water onto my lap. . . . My first instinct is to shake my child. "What's the matter with you? How can you be so clumsy?" I could just as well have said, "Don't worry. It was an accident. Let's clean it up together."

—Neil Kurshan,
Raising Your Child
to Be a Mensch

A parent once admitted to me, "When I get angry, I say things to my children that I wouldn't say to my worst enemy. I'm ashamed of the words that come unbidden out of my mouth!"

This was a cry from the heart. I could identify with it, having so often felt the same anguish when I would speak to my own kids in anger. Regardless of socioeconomic class, region, religion, or education, I regularly hear the same concern from parents who want to know how to handle their explosions of rage toward their children. These normally loving parents sometimes can't believe their own ears when they hear themselves jumping down their kids' throats. As book publisher and humorist Bruce Lansky once wrote, "The easiest thing to be consistent about in child rearing is losing your temper." Of course, this is a struggle for parents of one child as well as for parents of more than one. But I've found that sibling wrangling, meanness, and conflict can be one of the most powerful and frequent triggers for parental anger. Siblings definitely add fuel to the fire! And it's a lot easier to send one child to his room while you calm down than it is to extricate yourself from a crying baby and two older kids engaged in a popcorn fight. As one mother sighed, "Sometimes I'd like to shout, 'Okay, everybody into the barn!' But we don't have a barn."

I've noticed that when parents talk about their anger they grow quite somber, as though they are describing the ultimate betrayal of parental goodness. They're always looking for advice about how to stop being angry. But the issue is not whether or not parents are going to get angry sometimes—they are!—but what to do when the anger strikes. They need skills, not lectures.

I feel so strongly that anger is normal and inevitable and can be handled in a positive way that I wrote an entire book about it *(Love and Anger: The Parental Dilemma)*. After my book was published, I received many moving letters from parents confiding how relieved they felt to learn that they weren't monsters for feeling angry. Time and again, people remarked that they never thought they had any right to these feelings. They were convinced that "good" parents didn't lose their tempers. Some admitted they tried to keep their feelings buried so deep that it would take a major excavation to unearth them.

What Makes Parents Angry?

When I ask parents to talk about the disadvantages of having more than one child, the initial reaction is often discomfort. Although parents will readily admit that at times they feel overwhelmed and find it difficult to control their anger, they usually stop short of saying that there's anything negative about having more than one child, and it's even harder to get them to admit that they sometimes look back nostalgically to the days before number two or three or four arrived on the scene. They don't want to sound disloyal. However, once trust is established in a group and parents realize that it's a safe place to vent without being judged, they become very honest. And with that honesty comes a tremendous sense of relief. They told the truth and lightning didn't strike! The Parenting Police didn't show up at the door to drag them away.

Being honest about your feelings—even the uncomfortable ambivalence that every parent of two or more children sometimes experiences—can actually help you handle your anger. It's important to acknowledge (if not out loud, at least to yourself) that sometimes things are just too tough, and sometimes you wish you didn't have the life (or kids) you have, and sometimes you wish they would all go away and just leave you alone. When you can say openly that, yes, there are disadvantages to having more than one child, you're not negating your decision; nor are you demeaning your children. You're just being real.

In a recent workshop, after much discussion, the women in the group finally began to open up and speak frankly about their feelings. I think they were relieved after they allowed themselves to talk about the downside of having more than one, especially after realizing that they weren't alone.

Denise spilled out her list of disadvantages in one big breath: "It's so noisy, and there's never enough time to do everything. I'm often in the unenviable position of having to choose between changing a drippy diaper, testing my ten-year-old on his spelling, and scrubbing muddy footprints off the kitchen floor. Then my husband walks in the door after being at the office for ten hours and gets crazy because there's so much chaos." She rolled her eyes and laughed. "What have I forgotten? There's probably more."

"Well," added Debbie, "there's the huge extra expense. Does it sound too mercenary to mention that?"

"It's a simple fact that with two children, twice as much goes wrong," said Cynthia, the mother of two preschool-age twin boys. "There are twice as many sleepless nights, twice as many sick kids, twice as many mishaps, twice as many dirty clothes, twice as many tears, twice as many toys strewn all over the house, twice as much food that somebody refuses to eat or drops on the floor. And look at me. I must be a real glutton for punishment—I'm pregnant!"

Shirley, the mother of a six-year-old and a two-year-old, said with a lot of pain in her voice, "I feel myself getting very angry sometimes—resentful, really. My career went totally down the drain after my second son was born. It meant so much to me, but I just couldn't keep up a high-powered job and raise a toddler and a baby, too. Sometimes, when I'm talking to women from work, I feel so jealous, it goes right down to the tips of my toes. Although I try so hard to get excited about my kids' projects, I have to admit that often I'm just bored to tears. I long for the adult conversations at the office and the feeling of order and quiet. Then, when the kids start bickering and bopping each other, I just lose it and start yelling."

As you can see, parental anger is complicated. It's not just a matter of getting upset because your kids defy you, or blowing up when they whine and fight too much. More essentially, it's about expectations and disappointments, frustration and guilt. It's about wanting to protect your children from following dangerous paths and discovering that there is so much you can't control. It's about the desperate desire that your children be happy, and the daily reminder that happiness is a fickle friend. It's about the imperfections of life, the built-in flaws of human nature, and the barriers in the road to satisfaction and peace. More often than not, anger gets triggered by little things, catching you when you're tired, overworked, anxious, or just plain down in the dumps.

Take this simple example. Sharon's five-year-old daughter, Nicole, and her four-year-old son, Charles, are arguing over who gets to send for the free toy advertised on the back of the cereal box. It's a silly argument, like millions of others that occur every morning in America.

CHARLES: I wanted it first, so it's mine.
NICOLE: But you didn't say you wanted it. You have to say it or it doesn't count.
CHARLES: I put my finger on it.
NICOLE: Fingers don't count. Only saying counts.

SHARON: (finally interceding) Why don't we send for the toy
            and you both can share it.
CHARLES: No, it's mine.
NICOLE: I was the first one to say it.

"And on and on they went, continuing their totally witless argument," Sharon said. "Eventually, I got so angry that I grabbed the cereal box out of Nicole's hand and made a big production of tearing up the coupon and throwing it in the trash."

When I asked Sharon what bugged her most about that banal morning scene, she said, "It wasn't even the arguing. That's par for the course. It was the petty selfishness of it. My children were being such little brats. Their refusal to share disgusted me."

This incident reflects a common experience: A mundane little quarrel can send parents mentally spinning off into galaxies far beyond the breakfast table. Sharon's anger was triggered because she thought she caught a glimpse of negative qualities in her children that directly opposed her most cherished values. A typical breakfast squabble mushroomed (at least, in her mind) into a symptom of their moral decline. No wonder she got so mad!

It's amazing how these ordinary incidents can trigger such sudden flashes of rage, especially when you're exhausted and your kids just won't let up. If you've had a terrible day, your boss yelled at you, your bus was mobbed, you picked the line at the grocery store where everyone was paying in pennies, and you're developing a splitting headache, an unflushed toilet can be the breaking point. Your rage isn't really over the unflushed toilet or the toys spread across the carpet. It's over everything. Besides, you have more license when it comes to your kids. You can't send your boss to bed without his supper or take away the bus driver's TV privileges. You can't tell your co-worker she's grounded or assign your in-laws to time-out—even though you may dearly wish to. But your children are sitting ducks.

When your anger reaches the point where you finally do explode, you might feel a momentary release, but it's very fleeting. What's more, your rage may serve only to inspire reactive rage in your children. It's a simple truth that anger triggers anger. Yelling doesn't make you feel better if the result is your kids yelling back or sobbing, or slamming doors or saying hateful things. And then, after the fever has died down and you don't feel so angry anymore, you're left with self-recrimination, and that can be the most unpleasant consequence of all. One trick to managing your anger, especially when it seems way out of proportion to the crime, is to remember that any and all feelings are okay; it's the words and actions that get you into trouble. Give in to your feelings. Indulge them, no matter how ugly they are. Feelings are part of being human. At the same time, try not to take them out on your kids. I know that's easier said than done, but there are techniques to help you.

Being Angry without Doing Damage

Many parents have told me how their own parents expressed anger with hurtful, insulting words that were sometimes remembered as painfully as slaps. People recognize that although it's human to get upset and lose your cool (kids, after all, can be terribly provocative), there's sometimes a thin line between expressing anger in a way that provides relief and being physically or verbally abusive.

In spite of our best intentions, we sometimes just can't help reverting to what is most familiar—"losing it" and saying the hurtful things to our kids that were once said to us. After all, our only training for being parents comes from a very powerful set of teachers—our own parents. We may want to foster respect, but can end up engendering fear. The well-worn words and phrases come pouring back from our youth, and our parents' voices inadvertently possess us when we're pushed up against the wall:

"Don't you dare!"

"Who do you think you are?"

"You're just asking for it."

"After all I do for you . . ."

"That'll teach you."

"You'll never learn, will you?"

"Wipe that smile off your face . . . or else!"

"Get out of my sight!"

"You want to cry, I'll give you something to cry about."

"I find that at my weakest and most impulsive moments in dealing with my children, I rely on the methods I know best—those of my parents," admitted Sally, the mother of four. "Now I'm becoming aware of how I try to overcontrol my kids, constantly order them around, bug them about little things. I yell and occasionally spank them. It makes me feel lousy. I know when I react that way I'm on autopilot, but my anger and frustration sometimes get the best of me."

Even parents who resist the urge to use a negative, harsh, or authoritarian approach have mixed feelings about the results. Julie, a terrific mom in my workshop, was determined to raise each of her children with a strong sense of self-esteem. "I vowed when I became a parent that my children would never be afraid of me the way I was of my mother and father." She grimaced—a mixture of pride and regret. "And they're not!"

We talk a lot about anger in my parent workshops, and for many people, the abuses they experienced in childhood still rankle—making them all the more concerned about their own feelings of fury at their children.

For example, Irene, now forty-six and the mother of two teenagers, says she still smarts when she thinks about her father's sarcastic, insulting manner. "He thought nothing of calling us pigs, threatening to make us go eat in the garage, or even saying, 'Go play in the traffic,'" Irene said. "Imagine telling your kids to go play in the traffic!" She smiled wryly. "I guess he got the peace and quiet he wanted, though. We never fought around our father because we were scared as hell of him."

Frances, the mother of three, recalled how her parents often sent confusing signals about love and anger. "Our father, who had a strict German background, would spank us at the end of the day for the infractions our mother reported, and then he'd hug and kiss us and say,

'If I didn't love you, I wouldn't spank you.' I remember that those hugs and kisses hurt as much as the spankings. I didn't understand it, and as I grew older I began to resent how easily my father accepted as truth that spankings equaled love."

Many people grew up with fear as the primary mode of discipline and teaching. Actually, back then it was called "respect." But most kids learned that respect was just a code word for fear. They knew there was something wrong with this method, and vowed that they would be different with their children. The problem is, they never learned a viable alternative. The first time a child stamps his foot and screams, "No! I won't!" their fantasies of calm, loving discipline dissolve and before they know it, they're stamping their own feet and screaming back, "Yes, you will, too!"

Parents model the behavior they want from their children. For example, the father who turns a child over his knee and spanks him while shouting, "Don't you ever hit your brother!" is modeling the very behavior he's criticizing. If you insult or ridicule your kids because you don't like their behavior, what message does that send? Behavior is learned. If you express your anger with physical or emotional violence, that's the method your kids will learn. Numerous studies show that often children raised in abusive homes grow up to become abusers themselves. That's hardly surprising, since the way they learned to express rage was to hit. We, as parents, need to model more civilized alternatives. We don't want to teach by hurting. Sarcasm, put-downs, labeling, and disdain are verbal poison, just as violence is physical poison.

When I speak to groups of parents about discipline, there are always questions about spanking. Chances are, their own parents spanked them, and many vowed they would never do the same. They recall feelings of rage, humiliation, and helplessness. But other parents who once decried spanking are now saying that they're not so sure. As one concerned mother put it at a recent lecture, "Maybe our kids are getting into trouble today because we don't apply the back of our hand." And a number of parents nodded in agreement when a father stated, "I believe that as long as they live in my house, my children should abide by my rules, or be willing to take their lickings."

It is an instinctive reaction to want to punish someone who has done something wrong, and spanking is a simplistic solution based on our own rage and desire for control. But when you hurt your child in order to teach him a lesson, it's bound to elicit the desire for revenge. As one father reflected, looking back, "When my dad swatted me, all I could think of was how much I hated him and how much I wished I could get back at him somehow. I still remember those feelings of helplessness and humiliation, even though I don't even remember what I did to get spanked in the first place." To me, this man's comment is a convincing argument against spanking as a means of teaching.

This is my position on spanking: As a parenting technique, it's woefully ineffective. It's also a form of bullying—a big person hitting a little person because he still can. Some parents may argue quite passionately about the efficacy of spanking, but let's face it, how many parents spank their kids when they're feeling calm and rational? Physical punishment most often happens when parents are at their angriest.

If your goal is to teach your children cooperation, responsibility, and concern for others, you won't accomplish it by physical punishment. Children who are hit may learn not to repeat unacceptable behavior, but their motivation is fear, not a sincere desire to change their behavior. They won't learn positive ways of dealing with similar situations if the only model we provided is that of an adult using power over someone smaller and weaker.

Considering that there is an epidemic of child abuse in this country, I think the least we can do is declare a moratorium on hitting and spanking. As the caretakers of our children's futures, surely we can agree to discipline in more positive ways.

What to Do When You Feel Like Exploding

I've never met a parent who felt good about losing her temper with her children. Parents don't mean to yell, threaten, or hurt their children.

They know it often backfires. But knowing something in theory is a long way from being able to practice it in reality. Here are some techniques that may help.

❦ *Take a time-out.*

My favorite four-letter words when you are about to lose it are *exit* and *wait*. That's because you can be a little nicer than you feel, but not much. If your kids have managed to drive you ballistic, it's not realistic to expect that you're going to be able to engage them in any kind of rational dialogue. You—and they—need a time-out.

Grace, whose four-year-old son Andrew was having trouble adjusting to the presence of his baby sister, pushed Mom to the limit the day she walked into the kitchen and caught him standing on a stool emptying all the carefully filled formula bottles down the sink. "Andrew!" she shrieked. "What are you doing?" She stormed across the room, pulled him from the stool, and gave him a hard swat on his rear end. Then she shoved him toward the door. "Get out of my sight!" Andrew ran crying to his room. "As soon as Andrew left the kitchen, I noticed the pitcher of Five Alive on the counter," Grace said. "I realized that he was planning to fill the bottles with his favorite juice, and that it probably seemed like a very good idea to him. I was terribly upset at my impulsive reaction. I don't believe in spanking, but at that moment, I just couldn't stop myself. I went to his room to make sure he was okay, and through his sobs, Andrew choked out that he was just trying to fix bottles for his sister that weren't so icky. I kept saying, 'I know, I know, it's okay,' but it was a very upsetting incident."

Grace's anger sent her into automatic pilot—an impulsive state where she said and did things she regretted. We've all been there. But how might she have handled it differently? She could have marched into the kitchen, firmly pulled Andrew from the stool, and said, "I get very upset when I see the bottles I carefully prepared being emptied down the sink. Go to your room until I've calmed down, and then we'll talk about this."

It's also helpful to devise a mantra—self-talk you use when you're starting to feel the purple rage. Or find something you can do immediately to cool down: Swear in a foreign language, lock yourself in the bathroom and shout, call a sympathetic friend on the phone, run around the block. These techniques may sound simplistic—a variation on the old advice to count to ten. But they can work. Anger does diminish over time, just as boiling water does eventually cool down.

❧ *Talk about yourself, not them.*

When our children make us angry, we easily lapse into put-downs and attacks: "Why are you always so mean to your sister?" "Can't you kids ever say anything nice?" "What the heck is wrong with you?" "You boys are just like wild animals!" Statements like these communicate to our children that *they* are unacceptable, not their actions. It's more effective and less hurtful to make "I" statements. For example, instead of saying, "You're just like wild animals!" try "I can't concentrate on my driving with all this noise." Rather than, "Why are you always so mean to your sister?" say, "Calling your sister names is unacceptable. You'll have to find another way to express your anger." Instead of "You're driving me crazy," try "I need quiet right now."

Your tone of voice is crucial, as well. You're more credible when you speak strongly and firmly. Loud is okay if you keep it short. However, low tones are infinitely preferable to the high-pitched shriek that sometimes gets us when we're at our most vulnerable.

As I mentioned earlier, avoid generalities: "Be good." "Behave." "Act nice." "Don't argue." "Listen up." "Obey." "Knock it off." They don't really mean anything to your children. Instead, be specific about what you're asking them to do: "If you're going to argue about the puzzle, please do it out of earshot." Or, "I need to use the phone. Turn the radio down to the number two volume level."

❧ *Don't futurize.*

A mother in one of my workshops, bemoaning her son's poor performance on his high school entrance exam, said, "I can see the writing on the wall." She didn't have to explain what she meant. This expression called to mind permanent images of gloom and doom: her son dishing out hamburgers at McDonald's well into his forties, or huddled on a street corner sipping from a bottle of cheap wine, or confined to a prison cell. Many parents automatically project gloomy long-term scenarios whenever their kids disappoint them. And it is very common for parents to futurize negatively about sibling relationships. When they see their children behaving toward each other with pure nastiness, they convince themselves that this is the way it will always be—enemies forever. I can still remember the mother of a friend of mine who started sobbing when she came upon her children engaged in a particularly insulting verbal war. "I can't stand the thought that my children will be fighting at my funeral," she cried. Of course, since she was in her mid-thirties, her funeral was likely to be many years away, so this was an extreme case of futurizing.

When you're angry or disappointed with your children, try to stay in the present. Avoid saying things like, "At the rate you're going, you'll never amount to anything," or "Your sister will grow up hating you if you don't try to be nicer." Instead, address the issue at hand, preferably saying, "I'm disappointed in your report card," or "You're furious with your sister, but it's not acceptable to tear off her doll's head." Focus on the misbehavior of the moment, without assuming it's symbolic of the future.

Remember, our crystal balls are all cloudy. We don't know what's going to happen when our kids are grown. We barely know what to expect for tomorrow!

❧ Be brief and specific.

People often ask me, "What can I do when my children won't take no for an answer or always enlist me in a long debate? Usually, these scenes end with me yelling." Even though most parents have learned from experience that explanations and justifications usually end up in an argument, they should be aware that kids are never too busy for battle. From the age of about three many of them are accomplished arguers, ready to invest plenty of time and effort in trying to convince us to change our minds or convert a no into a yes. Sometimes, as the following example illustrates, their skills are impressive:

MOM: No cookies before dinner.

BILLY: Why not?

MOM: They'll ruin your appetite.

BILLY: No they won't. My appetite is as big as a house.

MOM: That's the rule. No cookies before dinner.

BILLY: But why?

MOM: They're not good for you.

BILLY: Yes they are. See, no fat!

And so on until Billy's frazzled mother yells, "I said no and I mean no. Quit arguing with me or I'm never bringing another cookie into this house!" (At which point Billy is likely to insist, "But Grandma lets me. . . .")

I feel great empathy for the parents who actually believe they can employ common sense and reason to convince their children that they don't really want what they want. When it comes to counterarguments, kids are models of patience, debaters ready for the Yale Law School. You can't win. The best strategy is to be firm and keep it simple:

"Cookies are for after dinner."

"No hitting."

"Time for bed."

"Let's go."

"The bus is coming."

"Mommy has to work now."

"No more TV. It's eight o'clock."

"No fighting while Mom is driving."

Children do not always require an explanation. Once in a while, it's okay to say, "Because I said so," or "Because I'm the parent." Sometimes it's the only honest answer.

🦋 *Put it in writing.*

This is one of the most effective ways for making your point in a calm, direct way. It's hard to remain furious when you're concentrating on putting your thoughts and feelings on paper. And children often respond better to a clear note or sign than to our strident voices.

Sue's ten-year-old son, Alex, was holding baby Jackie when she spit up all over his favorite shirt. He screeched and jumped off the sofa, dropping Jackie face down into the cushion. Sue was alarmed and angry because she had trusted Alex to be responsible when he was holding the baby. She pushed Alex away and yelled, "Go to your room!" as she rushed to soothe Jackie's cries. Later, when she was less upset, she decided that rather than lecture Alex about how irresponsible he was, she would write him a note. She thought Alex might take it more seriously, and she knew it was a safer way for her to control her anger and disappointment.

As Sue formulated her thoughts on paper, she became calmer and was able to work at making the incident a lesson for Alex, instead of a meaningless lecture. The result was this note:

> Dear Alex,
>
> I can see why you'd be upset when Jackie spit up stinky white goo on your favorite shirt. Babies do that sometimes, so it's always best to use a cloth or a diaper when you're holding them. It scared me when you dropped Jackie, and that's why I yelled. But I want you to know I appreciate how nice you are to your baby sister. She really loves it when you hold her. Let's plan to keep plenty of cloths handy for emergencies.
>
> Love, Mom

Alex appreciated the note and apologized for his unthinking behavior.

Ellen became very upset when her fourteen-year-old daughter kicked her younger stepbrother because she caught him in her room. "I lost it. I yelled, 'You selfish bitch!'—about the worst thing I could say. I don't even allow the word 'bitch' in my house. Carol ran to her room and didn't come out for the rest of the evening. At one point, I could hear her crying. I knew I couldn't tolerate Carol kicking her brother, but I regretted that I had been abusive." Before she went to bed that night, Ellen slipped this note under Carol's door:

Dear Carol,

    I'm sorry for yelling at you tonight. It upset me that you kicked Patrick. Kicking isn't the way we solve problems in this house. But neither is yelling, and I shouldn't have yelled— especially using a word I don't allow you to use. I know it isn't easy to have a new stepbrother in the house. You are entitled to some privacy, and it's frustrating when Patrick barges into your room uninvited. Let's discuss better ways to handle this dilemma. I welcome your ideas.

Mom

P.S. I love you!

The following afternoon, Ellen found this note on her bed:

Dear Mom,

    Please tell Patrick that my room is off-limits, and maybe give me a lock for the door if he won't listen. I won't kick or hit him, except in my mind. I love you, too, but I hate it when you yell.

Your daughter,
Carol

This example demonstrates another benefit of written memos and reminders. It encourages kids to write us back and gives them another way to express their thoughts and feelings. A mother I know still has the note her six-year-old son scrawled to her twenty years ago: "Dear Mom, Even when I'm mad and sad I still love you."

Sometimes written messages can be short and to the point. For Lee, the mother of three kids, six, seven and ten, the issue was simple: five minutes alone in the bathroom. Such a small thing, but for her a seemingly impossible goal. No matter how many times she begged and screamed or threatened, her kids always brought their arguments, complaints and questions to the bathroom door whenever she shut it behind her. Finally, she made a sign and posted it on the door:

A Message from Your Mother:
This is to announce that I will no longer be available for conversation or aggravation when I am in the bathroom. The door is closed and so are my ears. Thank you for your consideration.

The Head Honcho

Her kids got a big kick out of the sign, and it actually worked. The first couple of times they forgot and tried to talk to her through the bathroom door, Lee limited her reply to three words: "Read the sign." Eventually, they got the point.

❦ *Don't make rules you can't enforce.*

"I can't stand it when my kids use the word 'hate,' which they do regularly," Jan told me. "They're so nasty to each other! Always saying, 'I hate you,' or 'I hate you back.' When I was growing up, we were never allowed to say things like that and it still makes me very uneasy." Jan finally got so fed up she made the following rule and announced to her children, "In this house, we never say 'hate.'" Her fifteen-year-old daughter, the worst offender, accepted the rule without complaint, and simply found other ways to communicate her disgust with her younger brother. "I despise you," she told him. "You're a barf face. You're a pea brain." When Jan reminded her of the rule, her daughter gave her an innocent look and replied, "Oh, you never said I couldn't use the word 'despise.' And is 'pea brain' off-limits, too? You just said we couldn't say 'hate.'"

Kids have a maddening ability to be literal, so you have to be absolutely clear about your rules. And try not to make rules that are impossible to enforce. For example, kids are going to mouth off to their siblings no matter how often you tell them it's not allowed. One mother told the story of how her ten-year-old son called his older sister an "evil, ugly slug." She was appalled. "There will be none of that talk in this house!" she stated firmly, at which point her son boldly cried, "Evil, ugly slug!" She immediately sent him to his room. Five minutes later, as she passed his doorway, she heard whispering inside and pressed her ear to the door. In a very low voice, her son was saying over and over again, "Evil, ugly slug . . . evil, ugly slug . . . evil, ugly slug."

Clearly, this mother was fighting a losing battle by trying to enforce "nice talk" in her house. The best she could hope for was that her kids saved the worst taunts for when they were out of earshot. Understandably, parents who were raised in homes where "heck" and "darn" were the worst curses spoken will have trouble adjusting to the graphic language of today's youth. Thanks to TV and the movies, our children have a whole new selection of charming epithets—like Butt-head, Fart Breath, Wart Brain, and others too offensive to include here but that most of us have heard. Let's face it, profanity and vulgarity are a real problem today because the standard of what's acceptable has been so diluted by adult society. Words and phrases that would have sent our grandparents racing for the smelling salts are overheard everywhere. The current climate makes it so much harder for parents to limit vulgarity. But when you're trying to set rules, it might be helpful to distinguish between insulting curses that have become habitual and must be addressed, and rare expletives that spill out in moments of true frustration and may be better off ignored.

Whether you're establishing rules about language, curfews, chores, snacks, or any of the myriad issues that arise, be sure that you really mean it. If "no" is actually "maybe," or if you are inconsistent, your kids will catch you up on it, making matters worse than if there were no rule at all. Remember, kids love to use our words against us, and they delight in tripping us up in verbal debates. They also have lots of free time to do it. For most kids, engaging you in arguments and catching you in inconsistencies is lots of fun. It breaks the boredom. If you speak in absolutes, you're likely to hear:

- "You promised to be back in five minutes, and it's five minutes and thirty seconds. You always tell us never to lie, but you lie yourself."
- "You said wash up. You didn't say brush your teeth."
- "You let us go swimming after dinner yesterday. Now today you say it's not allowed."
- "You said no soda before bedtime, but you didn't say no Snapple. Snapple isn't soda."

🙖 *Make peace.*

In the aftermath of losing your temper, you probably feel somewhat deflated. Maybe you're thinking, "I did it again. I promised myself I wouldn't yell, but I screwed up." Before you launch too deeply into self-flagellation, consider these two facts: One, no parent, even the most loving, handles anger like a model adult every single time. Two, you always have another chance. Kids are resilient. And sometimes they're even understanding. Don't you think they realize how much they push your buttons? At the same time, after you've really blown your stack and gone ballistic, most children are eager to make up with you. In fact, they welcome the relief of knowing that even the most irate parent can feel loving once again. One mother shared this story of anger and resolution:

"No matter how good my intentions, I would always end up screaming in the morning. Then I'd feel terrible all day. It occurred to me that my kids were picking up their signals from me, and if I was calmer in the mornings, they would be too. So I had a talk with them and told them I wasn't going to scream anymore, and I hoped they would try to cooperate. Well, the very next morning, my good intentions went right out the window. The kids were running through the house naked while I was trying to get them to settle down and get dressed. I started yelling and dragging them to their rooms. My son was crying, and he said, 'I thought you said you weren't going to yell at us anymore.' Well, I felt so defeated and guilty. I sat down on his bed, put my head in my hands, and said, 'You're right. I really didn't want to yell anymore. So now what do you think I should do?' I was so distraught that I was really appealing to this six-year-old for the answer to my problems. And, to my surprise, he gave me one. He patted my arm as though he understood my frustration. 'Well,' he said, 'try again not to scream.' It was a sweet moment. He understood better than I did that people (even mothers!) aren't always perfect, and that we all get another chance."

Another mother had a similar experience during a quiet moment with her seven-year-old son. She knew how much trouble she had controlling her outbursts, especially during the morning rush hour, the most uptight time of the day for her. She kept reminding herself that being late wasn't the end of the world (trying to undo a message that had been drilled into her by her mother). She wanted to find ways of being more organized and less uptight, and she apologized to her son for so often being angry in the morning. He replied quite cheerfully, "Oh, that's okay, Ma. I know it's just your bad angle."

She was amazed by his answer. "The weight of the world flew off my shoulders," she said. "I felt so validated. Imagine that, at seven he already knows that being angry doesn't make you a bad person."

Chapter 8

Kids Tell Their Side of the Story

I like little brothers and sisters because if you're angry at a parent or something, you can go to them and give them a big hug, and they let you.

—Rachel, nine

Last year, I had an opportunity to conduct a workshop for young people at the Hudson School in Hoboken, New Jersey. Over the years, I've listened to thousands of parents tell me what it was like to raise more than one child, so I was eager to hear the kids themselves discuss their feelings about having siblings.

I arrived at the Hudson School not quite knowing what to expect. The principal, Suellen Newman, had assembled a group of boys and girls between the ages of nine and sixteen. All of them had brothers and sisters, and naturally they were glad to be called out of their regular classes to participate. But I felt a bit of trepidation. Frankly, I anticipated that our time together would deteriorate into a gripe session.

Not surprisingly, there was plenty of that. But I was also delightfully surprised to discover among these children a deep reservoir of pleasure at having siblings. I had the sense that even when they were describing the things that annoyed or angered them, there was an underlying acceptance of this being just the way it was supposed to be.

They really enjoyed our time together, and seemed to have fun venting and griping—but with a fundamental affection and warmth that was unmistakable in their smiles and enthusiasm. This dialogue was typical:

ASHLEY: I have two brothers. One is seven and one is five and a half. They're monsters.

ME: They're monsters? Oh. Anyone else have monster siblings?

TAMELAH: Oh, yes!

LORI: Their socks smell.

JEFFREY: Thanks. Thanks a lot. My socks do not smell.

This dialogue was followed by uproarious laughter. Nilmarie, nine, added, "My brother is sixteen and he treats me like a baby. He calls me shrimp and I hate that. And he's always torturing me."

"What does he do?" I asked Nilmarie.

"Well," she said, "like there's this huge sofa and everybody in the house loves sitting on the sofa. So when my brother sits on the sofa, I say, 'Mom wants you in the kitchen.' So he goes to the kitchen and I stretch out on the sofa. Then he comes back and throws me on the floor."

"I don't blame him!" I said.

"You think that's bad?" Anna, ten, interrupted eagerly. "I don't think so. My big brother does worse things, like holding me upside down until my face turns blue. He's eighteen. I'm telling you, big brothers are trouble."

The group launched into a passionate tirade against older brothers, younger brothers, older sisters, and younger sisters—vying for the position of most tormented. I sat back and noticed how much they were enjoying themselves. I got a kick out of watching their animated faces and the enthusiasm with which they launched into their complaints, each one wanting to outdo the others. Here was an enjoyable opportunity to vent that they probably didn't get at home.

I also noticed that their gripes were pretty mundane. There was little evidence of true, abiding hatred. In fact, moments after Anna proclaimed her eighteen-year-old brother to be the worst of all, she said, "Last month we took him to college, and I just had to go back into the car because I was crying. Because he was going to stay there for five months."

"You were really going to miss him," I said.

Anna nodded her head in wonder. "I was sobbing. I couldn't believe it. I mean, that's the brother that I fight with the most, that I kick, who beats me up. And there I am crying."

"Does that seem crazy to you?" I asked Anna. She shrugged. "No, because sometimes I like to tease him and it's fun when he teases me."

Several of the kids commented that older siblings were a piece of cake compared to younger siblings. Often, the complaint was that the younger ones got away with murder. Michael, eleven, was frustrated because his four-year-old sister seemed to get all the breaks while he got all the blame. I asked him for an example.

"Okay," he said. "She'll be lying on the bed and she'll fall off. And she goes and cries to our mom, 'Michael pushed me off the bed.'"

"Why do you think she does that?" I asked.

"She doesn't want to admit she's clumsy. So she blames me."

"What does your mother say?" I asked.

"Mom comes in and goes, 'Why did you push your sister?' and I'm like, 'No, I didn't.' But she believes my sister. Then I get punished, like I can't watch TV for a while."

"That must get you pretty mad," I said sympathetically.

Michael smirked. "Yeah. I get back at her, though. Like, when we play, I trip her occasionally." His reply produced giggles from the group. Kids appreciate the justice of reciprocity.

We talked for an hour, each child delighting in his or her complaints about siblings. But as our time together drew to a close, I asked the kids if there were good things about having siblings. Everyone agreed that having more than one child was best. "I had a friend who was an only child," Alex said. "And he was pampered beyond belief. He had nothing to do when he was at home. At least when I get home, there's brothers and sisters to scream at. I'm like deaf when my brother is blasting his stereo beyond all hell." And that seemed to sum things up perfectly.

Why did I decide to solicit the kids' side of the story? It was not my intention to give parents more things to feel guilty about. I didn't want to add a new list of complaints about brothers and sisters. What I hoped for—and succeeded in getting—was a positive, even forgiving perspective.

As the children at Hudson School demonstrated, kids are capable of moving easily between complaint and appreciation in the blink of an eye. While parents torture themselves with the horrible things their children say and do to one another, and imagine them growing up as lifelong enemies, the children themselves are often having the time of their lives bickering and plotting and, finally, loving each other.

Children can help parents lighten up and let go of their guilt. For example, the children I've talked to are almost unanimous in their belief that it is better to have siblings than to be only children—in spite (and even because) of the fighting, competition, and the reluctant sharing. In their refreshing way, kids are able to take things in stride that make their parents' hair stand on end. And that's a great lesson for the harried parent. I believe that the candid insights of the children themselves provide a terrific antidote to guilt, and I encourage you to read them whenever you start to question your sanity for having more than one child.

Kids Have Plenty to Say about Siblings

In addition to conducting workshops with kids, I also developed a questionnaire which many children have filled out (with and without the help of parents). This questionnaire (see Appendix C) was something of an afterthought to the one I developed for parents. I felt it was a good exercise for the children, and might help parents see sibling battles in a new light. But I wasn't sure whether the children would want to spend time answering such a questionnaire. To my delight, responses flooded in from children of all ages. Their replies were honest, funny, and sometimes touching. I'd like to share some of the questions and the kids' unedited answers.

🌤 *How do you feel about having brothers and sisters?*

As I expected, there was plenty of ambivalence about having siblings. Responses ranged from "It's yucky. I hate it" to "It's cool." Most fell somewhere in between, like the seven-year-old who answered, "Medium."

Monique, twelve, wrote this about her ambivalence: "What is good about siblings? They yell and fight. They borrow your things. Get you in trouble. Sometimes they can be cute, like when they are nice to the lady on the street. When they think of you, I guess they love you but don't always know how to show it."

Here are some of the other responses:

"I like it and I don't like it. I like having someone around, but sometimes we fight and I don't like that."

TAYLOR, eleven

"I'm glad I have someone around to do things with. Only children probably get lonely. But they tag along too much and get annoying sometimes."

ABIGAIL, fourteen

"I feel not so lonely."

DANA, eight

"Sometimes happy, sometimes mad."

WHITNEY, twelve

"My older sister comforts me and teaches me and is nice."

JULIA, eleven

"It feels terrible."

RAUL, eight

"A little bit bad."

MAISIE, six

"When my sister was born I was really happy because I used to have imaginary friends and when she was born it was like they vanished into thin air."

RACHEL, nine

"My brothers and sisters annoy me and take all my stuff."

J.D., six

"I like it. You have built-in friends and always have someone to confide in."

MERILEE, twelve

"Ninety-nine percent of the time it is extremely annoying, but sometimes it can be quite useful."

EDWARD, thirteen

"It's fun to have a younger sister because I can tease her."

OLIVER, ten

"At first when she was born I was excited, but now she gets in my way too much."

JUSTINE, six

"It's very hard because they push you around a lot. They think because they are older they can do whatever they want, and most of the time you can't do anything about it."

ALEX, twelve

"Sometimes it's fun to have someone to play with, but if you have an older sibling it usually ends up with a fight."

MARISSA, nine

"Good. She drives me crazy. She plays with my toys. When she laughs I like it."

SIMON, six

"I like them. They are good company. Most only children I know are kind of nerdy."

STEPH, eighteen

"The best thing is having someone to talk to when I'm feeling sad. I'm in the middle which is lucky because I have a sister on either side of me. One I can look up to and the other I can help. But sometimes we fight and get punished."

PERRIN, nine

&ra; *What do you fight about?*

The kids seemed to relish the chance to answer this question. They also displayed a sense of humor about it—which should be a comfort to the parents who fear that sibling squabbles might lead to permanent enmity. Listening to the children describe their fighting behavior, I was more convinced than ever that sibling fights are a normal part of family life that kids accept with more equanimity than we give them credit for.

Some issues appeared repeatedly. You know what they are: the front seat, TV, toys, privacy. Many admitted that they fight the most about "dumb stuff," "stupid things," or as thirteen-year-old Edward cheerfully responded, "Anything that comes into our heads." Here are some of their answers to the question, "What do you fight about?"

"Almost everything."

OLIVIA, eight

"Lately, we don't fight very much. But one of my sisters doesn't know how to keep her mouth shut. We have different opinions on different subjects and different personalities."

ABIGAIL, fourteen

"You name it, we fight about it."

JEFF, fourteen

"Clothes, TV, sports, food, people, gifts, money, music, and opinions."

ERIN, sixteen

"Usually something little, then we forget why."

JAMIE, ten

"When we play hockey and I make a goal and my brother says it's not a goal."

MIKEY, eight

"We fight about toys and sometimes we fight for no reason."

RACHEL, nine

"If someone by accident hits the other."

WILLY, ten

"About playing games and races and jumping on Mommy's bed."

DANA, four

"Different things. For example, when my brother owes me something but he doesn't agree. Also, during sports when he cheats. Or when he teases me."

TYLER, eleven

"Who uses the bathroom."

ZACHARY, twelve

"We fight about taking each other's things, and we also fight about how sometimes they call you a copycat or something like that and you get angry because you know you're not."

ALEX, twelve

🙶 *Do you ever tattle to get a sibling in trouble? What happens when you do?*

To this day, I remember that one of my mother's most consistent rules was "The one who tattles gets punished." Since I was the main tattler in my family, a victim of my older brother's torment, I thought this rule was dreadfully unfair. It left me feeling unprotected when I really did need help. But it also robbed me of the pleasure I took in getting my brother in trouble. I was surprised to find that my mother's rule was fairly typical in the households of the children who answered the questionnaire. Even those children who did get away with tattling acknowledged that the consequences weren't always worth it. Maisie, six, said that she sometimes told on her older brother, "but then I don't have anyone to play with." Jeff, fourteen, said that while telling on his brother gave him some satisfaction, "he always gets back at me."

These are some of the kids' comments about tattling:

"I do get my brother into trouble, but nothing happens to me."

OLIVIA, seven

"If I do, I just get myself in trouble."

DANA, eight

"Yes, then I get in trouble because I'm the oldest."

WHITNEY, twelve

"I almost never do, most of the time. The time I did I got into trouble."

GABRIELA, sixteen

"Not anymore. Used to."

PAUL, thirteen

"I usually don't, but if someone in our house tattles, my sister calls them a tattletale."

RACHEL, nine

"It's not worth it to tattle. Nothing would happen. My parents just laugh."

DIANA, sixteen

"Sometimes. Mom says work it out."

AMANDA, eight

"The person who is tattling gets in trouble for tattling."

DARIN, twelve

"On occasion, but mostly out of revenge. Sometimes they get punished. It depends on the parents' mood."

PATRICK, thirteen

"I only tattle when I really get hurt. My brothers say I only did it to get them in trouble. Sometimes I do, but most of the time it's just to get back at them for hurting me."

ALEX, twelve

"When I tattle, my parents don't care, but they do when my sister tattles."

TRAVIS, thirteen

"I don't because since I'm the oldest my mother says, 'I can't believe you're fighting with a four-year-old,' and takes her side."

KATE, eleven

" 'Don't tattle,' is what my mom said. If we do, we usually lose TV for a night or two. Or we have to go to bed a half an hour earlier."

DANIELLE, eleven

"No. If we side with anyone, it's the two of us against our parents."

ALEXANDRA, seventeen

❧ *Do your parents play favorites or take sides?*

I expected this question to inspire a lot of passion. Favoritism is one of kids' common complaints. To my surprise, most of the responses were flat-out denials. There were, however, a few dissenters. Many children perceived that the youngest was most favored and got away with the most.

Here are some of their responses:

"Yes. They think we both torment the middle child. They don't bother seeing what she does to us. We must have a motive!"

KATE, eleven

"No, but they expect more of me and they should because I'm older."

DARIN, twelve

"My mom is always on my brother's side and my dad is always on mine."

TYLER, eleven

"Both my parents favor my little sister."

EMILY, ten

"Yes!!!"

PATRICK, thirteen

"Definitely not."

RACHEL, nine

"Jake gets away with murder."

JAMIE, ten

"Sometimes it seems like they jump in to help the underdog. (I'm the oldest so I'm never the underdog!)"

ABIGAIL, fourteen

❧ *What is the worst part of having siblings?*

Kids seemed to relish the chance to answer this question, and their responses covered the typical terrain of routine life—privacy, "stuff," sharing, and general aggravation. While parents often get annoyed hearing these complaints voiced, they should be relieved that remarks like "too many people at the dinner table" and "they bother you" were the most horrific answers kids could come up with. I was surprised at the lack of venom. It seemed that most of the children accepted annoyances as coming with the territory of having siblings. Their responses were hardly grist for a lifetime of hatred!

"Not having enough privacy."

TAYLOR, eleven

"When they aggravate you."

DANA, eight

"We fight a lot and they try to steal my friends."

WHITNEY, twelve

"They annoy me."

JAKE, seven

"Fighting, hitting, pinching, pulling hair, scratching, biting."

GABRIELA, sixteen

"The unjust arguments."

PAUL, thirteen

"You don't get all the attention."

JULIA, eleven

"When he takes my toys and when he grabs something from me."

CAROLINE, five

"She always comes into my room. She always calls me names. I usually get in trouble with my dad and she doesn't get in any trouble."

JULIA, eight

"Getting blamed for what you don't do. Having to share."

ABIGAIL, twelve

"I hate my brothers when they're mean to me."

KATHARINE, four

"Unfairness when someone gets favored."

KYLE, twelve

"They beat you up."

TYLER, eleven

"Well, they're always nagging you and bothering you and I don't like that."

ASHLEY, ten

"I hate having to see so many people when I want to be alone."

ALEX, twelve

"He embarrasses me in front of my friends."

MARISSA, nine

"She calls me a baby."

TOBIAS, six

"When she kicks and fights and pulls out my toys and calls me names."

SOPHIE, five

"I get the smallest allowance."

GEOFFREY, eight

"Sharing Mom and Dad with her."

EDWARD, thirteen

"She hurts me by running over my toes with her walker."

SIMON, six

"It always seems in the parents' eyes that the other one is right."

KATE, eleven

❧ *What is the best part of having siblings?*

Grievances were quickly shelved when kids answered this next question—or that's the way it appeared from their replies. It's impossible to read the following comments without believing that deep down, most kids really treasure their siblings—at least part of the time!

"You always have someone to be with."

ANNA, ten

"I like having commotion around the house."

KATE, eleven

"When you ask them to do something and they do it."

JULIA, four

"That they are like best friends."

PERRIN, nine

"Everything."

STEPH, eighteen

"She loves me."

TOBIAS, six

"I'm never lonely."

GEOFFREY, eight

"Being able to talk to them if you're ever in desperate need."

ALEX, twelve

"They always love you."

MONIQUE, twelve

"If somebody is being mean to you they'll beat them up."

ASHLEY, ten

"Laughing, secrets, sticking up for each other."

TAMELAH, eleven

"When he's nice, he teaches me things."

TYLER, eleven

"I love to tell them jokes and they are a lot of fun. They read to me and snuggle at night."

DANA, four

"You're never bored. There's always someone."

KYLE, twelve

"There's somebody else to take the attention away if I do something wrong."

PATRICK, thirteen

"Being able to annoy her."

EDWARD, thirteen

"Sometimes they bring you a lot of joy."

J.D., six

"I'm not lonely and they're there for me. They make me feel better when I cry or I'm not okay."

ILANA, six

"I think when she gets older she'll be better than she is now."

JULIA, eight

"Having someone else who's a lot like you helps you figure things out, confirm things, advise you."

ALEXANDRA, seventeen

"He's cuddly and keeps me company in the night."

CAROLINE, five

"Secrets and planning."

JULIE, seven

"Because."

JEFF, fourteen

"Picking on. Getting in bed with them."

CAITLIN, seven

"Since they are closer to your age than your parents are, they understand your problems better."

JULIANA, twelve

When you're grown and have a family, would you have more than one child?

When I first posed this question there were grunts, groans, and giggles, as if the kids could hardly imagine such a faraway scenario. But I believe this question was a true test of how kids felt about siblings. Of all the many responses, only one child answered that he didn't want more than one child. No matter how great their complaints, these children believed that having brothers and sisters was valuable. Many of them felt that having siblings was a basic part of what it meant to be a family. Their responses can be read as a big "Hooray!" for siblings:

"I'll have three, so if one of my children fights with another one, he'll still have someone to play with."

MARISSA, seven

"Yes, because I want to learn how to be a good mom."

CAITLIN, seven

"Yes, because if you only have one child that child never learns how to share."

JEFF, fourteen

"I think that a big family is important because it shows people how to deal with real situations. It helps people communicate their feelings."

ERIN, sixteen

"I think it might be more exciting."

DANA, eight

"More than one. I don't know why."

JAKE, seven

"I'd have two or three because I want to see rivalry from a mom's point of view."

JULIE, seven

"I want two kids because with three there's always the odd one out, and you can't fit four kids in the back seat of a car. Only children can be very lonely. Two kids keep each other company."

GABRIELA, sixteen

"Yes, because there are more pros than cons in having siblings."

PAUL, thirteen

"Yes, so I can take them places and they won't be bored."

MIKEY, eight

"More than one. I would have two. Because I like it better."

MAISIE, six

"I would probably have three children because one would be lonely. With two, if they got into a fight, there wouldn't be anyone to play with. But three would be perfect to me."

RACHEL, nine

"I'd have at least three, maybe four, because I'd want them to have the same feeling that someone's always there like I do."

KYLE, twelve

"I want two because if you have an only child, the child might get spoiled and be a brat."

ASHLEY, ten

"Yes, because only children are weaklings."

STEPH, eighteen

"Yes, definitely. I would hate having only myself. Kids need siblings!"

ABIGAIL, twelve

Kids Can Have Empathy for Parents

Recently, I was invited to speak in Nanaimo, British Columbia. While there, I visited Mountain View Elementary School, at which some teachers had interviewed their students on the topic of parenting. Instead of focusing on the experiences of the kids themselves, the teachers turned the tables a bit by asking students from different grade levels to list what were the hardest things about being a parent.

Their answers showed remarkable insight:

- Coming home from work and doing *more* work.
- Listening to kids fighting.
- Putting up with the noise.
- Cleaning up after the kids.
- Having kids around when you're trying to work.
- Stress and teenagers.
- Not getting enough help around the house.
- Trying to put us to bed.
- Coming home from work to find a mess and a stack of bills.
- Keeping everyone happy.
- Not having time for yourself.
- Stopping your kids from talking back.
- Doing everything for your kids and they don't care.
- Not having time to go out and have fun.
- Cleaning, cooking, and working.
- Working full-time and all the time.
- Putting up with irresponsible children.
- Putting up with teenagers, especially moody teenagers.
- Listening to kids fighting.
- Taking care of four children and a dog.

It seemed that most of the children understood that being a parent was one of the hardest jobs there was—especially when there was more than one child. (Only two were without siblings.)

Later, the sixth-grade teacher decided to turn the question into a writing assignment, and I felt privileged to read what the children had written. Here are some excerpts that impressed me.

Hillary, a girl with a twin brother, wrote her piece "pretending to be a stressed-out parent writing a letter."

Dear whoever you are,

It is hard being a parent because every day after a hard day at work all I want to do is sit down and relax, but as soon as I get home I have to do the dishes, make dinner, and do the laundry. I don't mind doing all this, but my children *never* offer to help. Instead, after having two feet inside the door, they ask me to drive them here and drive them there. Of course, I say yes and when I drive them I hardly ever hear a thank-you.

I have twins, one boy and one girl, and they are twelve and going through puberty. *This very moment!!!* Got to go.

Signed, Confused

Jessica, one of three children, wrote sympathetically,

Being a parent has got to be tough, can't you imagine? (You should be able to if you're a parent.) At the rate new cups are used in my house, my parents do the dishes at least fifty times a week. And laundry. That one's a major time waster. Especially when kids change often each day. Putting up with kids nagging, complaining, and fighting ought to be hard to put up with, too. Especially after work. Sometimes parents probably think they should work a late shift so they don't have to come home to hear kids doing their usual bickering routine. Do the three words, "Give it back!" sound familiar?

Michelle, who had one brother, echoed other kids' viewpoints when she wrote:

Dear Parents,

I think you have a hard time putting up with us kids. You're happy when you first have us, then we start to grow up. First we need new clothes. And when we are babies we keep you up at night. Then we want name brand CD players and, of course, Game Boy. We like to mess things up, but then again, we don't clean it up so you end up cleaning up. When we're teenagers, it's hard on you because we go through puberty, your phone bill is very high, and we want a raise in our allowance. Of course, we don't do enough chores. And Caleb won't put the toilet seat down. So I think I have a pretty good idea how you feel.

Ryan struck a nerve with the simple observation that "being a parent would be hard because the kids might like getting up early while the parent likes to sleep in." And Avery, while sympathetic, noted, "It's soooo hard being a parent, but look on the bright side. At least you're too young to be a grandparent!"

Jackie, one of four, wrote one of the most original essays. She imagined herself as the harassed parent of seventeen children!

Hello, my name is Amelia Cornerwitch. I am a parent of seventeen little brats. Now, I'll tell you how a normal day goes and how hard it is to be a parent! My day usually begins with having to wake up the kids and then make their breakfast. For breakfast I have to make seventeen bowls of cereal. I don't mind that so much, it's just having to clean up after all of them. First of all, cleaning up seventeen spoons and bowls, then spilt milk and juice. After breakfast, the kids get washed, brush their teeth and go to the bathroom. While they're doing that, I make their sandwiches for lunch, which is made up of thirty-four slices of bread, bologna, and about fifteen feet of Saran wrap. Finally, everybody is loaded into the truck and we're off to school. Well, when I get home I still don't get a minute's peace. First, I have to wash the boys' toothpaste and spit and the girls' lipstick off the mirror and the counter, and put all the toilet seats down in the house. After that mess I get to eat my lunch. After lunch I have to vacuum the carpet because of all the furballs from the cat. After that, I get ten minutes of peace before I have to pick up the kids. Then I make them do their homework while I make dinner. Well, the kids are total slobs, so by the time dinner is finished there's spaghetti noodles on the ceiling, floors, walls, and on the bottoms of the chairs. While the kids watch TV and then go to bed, I clean up the kitchen and finally go to bed. Then I wait for another day to come.

It's not often that kids say thanks or express appreciation for a parent's hard work and sacrifices. I imagine these children still go home at night and make demands, criticize their parents' decisions, neglect their chores, and sulk about unfairness. But it's heartwarming to know that in the deep recesses of their minds, they see just how tiring, tough, and complicated it can be to raise children.

Chapter 9

Let's Lighten Up!

Mother Murphy's Best Advice:
1. Hope for the best.
2. Prepare for the worst.
3. Love them no matter what.

—Bruce Lansky

"There's no joy in Mudville," Carol announced tiredly to my workshop group one morning. To look at her, it would seem that she had a point. Since the previous week, her eyes had sprouted deep worry lines. Her mouth was set tight, the corners turned down.

"You sound like you've had a rough week," I said.

"Shoot me now and put me out of my misery," she replied, and she wasn't laughing.

Carol went on to relate the dreary saga of life with twin toddlers and a five-year-old. "The little ones are like a Greek chorus of 'no's' and 'mines,' and my older daughter thinks that gives her permission to be obstinate, too," she said. "Is it too much to ask that just once someone in that house will do something—anything—I want? I'm not unreasonable. I'm just talking about putting on shoes, eating at least two bites of dinner, and going to sleep without getting back up a dozen times."

I thought Carol made perfect sense, and everyone else in the room thought so, too. Why couldn't parents get a break once in a while? I noted that the group seemed particularly grumpy that day. "Being a parent makes other jobs look like a breeze," I said, and no one argued. The mood seemed to drop another notch on the misery scale. Finally I said, "Everyone is so grim this week, when you walked in I thought maybe someone had died, or lost their fingers and toes or got bitten by a snake." Only then did they laugh. Sometimes I practically have to shake parents and yell, "Lighten up!"

The parents who come to my workshops really take the job seriously—that's why they come. They want to be the best parents they can be, but often I see that they take on the task like a heavy mission, to the point that, as Carol put it, "There's no joy in Mudville." What a pity that the very process of trying so hard can rob parenting of much of its joy.

Randall, a very gentle and serious young man who attended one of my workshops, was completely baffled by the vigor and vindictiveness with which his two sons fought. "I always wanted a brother," he said wistfully in the group one day. "I want my sons to cherish each other, not despise each other."

I asked Randall what he normally did when his sons fought. "I try to explain to them that fighting is not the right way to solve problems," he replied. "I try to use analogies to teach them. Like the other day, they were arguing over what constituted the exact middle of their room. They wanted to build a cardboard wall at exactly the middle point, but they couldn't agree on what the middle was. I tried to talk to them about what happens when people build walls. I used the Berlin Wall as an example . . ."

At that, Rhoda, a seasoned mother of four, burst out laughing. "You've got to be kidding!" she cried. "The Berlin Wall!"

Randall looked offended. "What's so funny?"

"I'm sorry for laughing," Rhoda said, "but it seems to me that a more appropriate response to that particular argument would have been, 'Wait, guys, I'll go get a tape measure.'"

Sometimes parents, like Randall, take the job so seriously, that they feel compelled to turn every incident into a lesson detailing the wisdom of the ages. They forget that there are many ways to teach, including doing nothing at all. I often tell parents, "Don't just do something, stand there!" It's another way of saying that you don't have to conscientiously work at manufacturing pearls of wisdom for every occasion. Yes, there *are* occasions when the most memorable response is actually the silliest.

What's the Worst Thing That Could Happen?

The best advice about lightening up often comes from parents who have three children or more. Once they've chucked the mantle of perfect parent—which usually happens out of necessity—they're able to ease up.

"I used to worry about every little thing when I had one," related the mother of four. "With my second child, I was still trying to be in perfect control—right down to interceding with lengthy sermons each time they argued. Now I've given it up. I let them fight their own battles and resolve things on their own because I just don't have the time or energy to do otherwise." She grinned. "And if they insist on slinging insults and bickering, I have a rule, 'Not here where I can hear.' And guess what? Things work out better without my intervention. It took having four children to learn what I wish I'd known with two."

Another mother, when asked how she managed to get four children dressed and off to school on time, answered without a hint of guilt, "Easy. They go to bed with their school clothes on."

One mother of three said without guilt, "We have learned to lower our standards about most things. And my husband and I have a rule: If no one is bleeding or sobbing, we're ahead of the game."

Another mother grinned when she told my workshop group, "There's a saying in our house that dinner is ready when the doorbell rings."

The other parents looked blank. They didn't understand what she meant.

"You know," she said. "Takeout!"

Many parents complain about what their children wear to school. It's embarrassing when your daughter dresses in as many layers as a Peruvian Indian. You just *know* people are out there thinking, "Haven't these people ever heard of the Gap?" One father who was in charge of getting two kids dressed every morning decided his daughter's strange taste in clothing was not a place to do battle. He did, however, ease his pangs of embarrassment by sending a note to the teacher: "Alice's fashion choices are a reflection of her unique taste, not the taste of her parents."

On a more serious note, Melinda, a very savvy mother of two, said, "Without question, the sheer logistics of raising two children blots out the tendency to be 'perfect' as a parent. Things that shouldn't become life-and-death issues don't. I think having multiple children forces us to adopt a saner, more rational approach to parenting because we have neither the time nor the resources to hand-craft the perfect child."

One day a group of mothers was solemnly discussing the value of spending "quality" time with their preschoolers. The consensus seemed to be that, as bored as they were by pushing trucks along the floor, playing Candyland, or building Lego spacecraft, these activities were somehow sacred—deemed essential for purposes of bonding with their children. Suddenly, one mother's voice rose above the others. "I'm sorry," she proclaimed defiantly. "I'm very clear about this with my older daughter. I just tell her, 'I don't play Barbies.' "

The nonapologetic nature of her remark stopped everyone in their tracks. Her words felt almost scandalous, but once spoken they were like a breath of fresh air. We began to talk about what "quality time" really meant. Those of us who had ever secretly skipped pages while reading stories or used occasional bribery because it was expedient, or deliberately lost at checkers to get the game over with more quickly felt free to say what we had always believed privately: Quality time by definition can be so stressfully full of "shoulds" and "oughts" that you lose the feeling of doing something mutually enjoyable.

Sometimes the best time with kids is when there's not that element of obligation or sacrifice. Spontaneous moments of pleasure feel more meaningful than hours devoted to blocks and Barbies and baseball cards and four books at bedtime. As someone once said, "Joy can be better caught than taught."

Take Time Out to Play

As parents, we see our job as teaching and directing our children. We are adults and we no longer inhabit their world of play and imagination. Our lives are busy with more serious matters of putting food on the table, getting teeth brushed, supervising homework, laundering clothes, and making sure no one gets an eye poked out when our backs are turned.

In contrast, our children's major goal is to have fun, and that often means wanting to do the opposite of what we want or need them to do. It's fun to dawdle and daydream instead of getting dressed in a rush. It's fun to stop and examine a spider crawling on the curb instead of hurrying across the street while the light is green. It's fun to push all the food on the plate into one mushy mountain and pretend it's a volcano with gravy dribbling from the top. It's fun to stay up later than the prescribed bedtime. It's fun to jump into every mud puddle on the street. It's fun to blow milk and juice bubbles through the bottom of straws instead of sedately sipping it. It's fun to play Monopoly for three hours straight, then beg for more. Children have endless patience for fun. Often adults just want to get the job done.

"I always loved kids until I had two of my own," one mother admitted wryly. "I enjoyed their imagination and creativity. But now I bite my tongue not to hurry my kids along, and I grit my teeth and try to smile when I have to answer their endless convoluted cosmic questions. When my three-year-old asks, 'Why do bees sting?' I want to snap, 'I don't know. Now put on your socks,' but I try not to. I'm ashamed to say I feel annoyed rather than charmed and delighted."

I can understand her feelings. It's not easy to stop and smell the roses when dinner's burning on the stove, the laundry is on the spin cycle, and you've got three messages to return on your answering machine. It's not even a good time to pretend to. There's a time and a place for everything, even roses.

But for a nonemergency, you might take an opportunity to lighten up on the schedule. One parent struck a nerve when she suggested that the reason kids dawdle at bedtime is because they never really feel they have us. We're always moving them along on the conveyor belt of the day. "It suddenly struck me, what's the big deal if I give them an extra fifteen minutes," she said. "Rushing them didn't work anyway. I can't do it every night, but if I can just loosen up and remember that the extra time might help us both relax, it makes such a difference. Oh, and the rocking chair has been a great addition for us all."

This parent's comment reminded me of the reason I get upset when parents are exhorted by experts to always be consistent. Certainly, it's a worthwhile goal, especially in enforcing structure and routines. But if parents take such advice too seriously, they don't give themselves permission to be flexible or easygoing when the occasion permits.

Learning to Lighten Up

Like everything else about parenting, the ability to take the job less seriously doesn't come easily. You need skills, and they can be hard to come by. Most of what we read and learn about parenting is focused on the depth and breadth of our responsibilities, not on trying to ease up on ourselves and our kids. That's a shame because learning to lighten up, and to find humor and laughter wherever possible, can make everything else much easier—and teach the important lessons, too. Here are some practical methods that parents say really work. Try them with your kids and you might be surprised at the results.

✿ *Catch your kids off guard.*

Cora, the mother of two elementary school boys and a four-year-old girl, worked full-time as a nutritionist at a local hospital. Although she usually felt completely exhausted by the time she dragged herself home from work in the evening, paid the baby-sitter, and threw on some comfortable slippers, she always took time to prepare a nutritious meal for her children—even though her temptation was to pack them in the car and head for the nearest Burger King, or throw some hot dogs into the microwave. "I would be a hypocrite if I didn't feed my kids properly after I spend the day lecturing other people about healthful eating habits," Cora explained. It was a constant source of frustration for her that her children didn't appreciate her efforts. In fact, they complained loudly about her dinner menus.

One night Cora came home from work feeling lousy. She thought she might be getting the flu. She collapsed on the couch, and when her children came into the room to ask about dinner, she found she couldn't summon the strength for a nutritional lecture. "How about chicken?" she asked tiredly. They groaned in unison. "Okay," she said, closing her eyes, "why don't we have Twinkies."

Cora was amazed when her three junk food lovers didn't race for the cookie bin. Instead, they stood and gaped at her in awe until her oldest son finally said, "Oh, Mom, don't be silly. Twinkies aren't dinner."

Cora frowned. "Hmmm . . . well, I had decided this was a no-cooking night, so what will we do?"

The children were silent, not daring to spoil the moment. After a decent interval, Mom sighed loudly. "I guess we'll just have to order pizza," she said. "I hope you don't mind too much. I know you were so looking forward to chicken and broccoli."

The kids found this hilariously funny, of course, and they were delighted with the unexpected meal suggestion from their nutritionally correct mom. They all gorged happily on pizza, and the next night there wasn't a peep of complaint about dinner.

Don't get me wrong. I am not suggesting that nutrition isn't important (although I have heard tales of children whose parents swear they ate nothing but peanut butter and spaghetti for a year and managed to survive). The point of lightening up is not to throw out your standards. It's to maintain flexibility, to let your kids see that you're willing to bypass the hard and fast rules under certain conditions. It's also a good way to teach them that few things in life are really so urgently important that they can't be set aside in times of need.

When a parent responds unexpectedly, it can baffle and charm children. Kevin, the father of two boys, said he and his younger brother still enjoy telling "The Birdbath Story" to anyone who will listen. "My mother's birdbath was her pride and joy," he said. "It sat in the middle of our backyard like a little shrine, and at the center was a large statue of Saint Francis of Assisi, the patron saint of the animals. One day, my brother and I were kicking a ball and it hit the statue and knocked Saint Francis's head right off. The head shattered in pieces, so there was no gluing it back on. We were doomed! Of course, it was unthinkable to confess our crime, but we knew that once the headless statue was discovered, our own heads were mush."

For days, the brothers fretted and squirmed waiting for discovery, but nothing happened. "It was impossible that our parents didn't notice. That headless Saint Francis was a glaring centerpiece in our backyard. But nothing was said. A week went by. Silence. This was driving us crazy," Kevin remembered. "It was ruining our lives. Finally, one night at dinner, my brother cracked. He shouted in a very loud voice, 'What about the birdbath?' I froze in terror. My parents looked blasé. My mother simply said, 'Oh, yes. You know, you boys should be more careful about where you throw your balls. Or maybe we should move the birdbath.' That was it."

Kevin said that the best part of the story was that almost twenty years later, their mother revealed that she had set them up. She saw them break the statue and she wanted to throttle them. But she decided to try an unexpected reaction, and it really did drive the boys crazy waiting for the moment of truth. To this day, the birdbath story is recalled at almost every family reunion, and it provides a sense of mutual hilarity.

❧ *When all else fails, try the absurd.*

Jane's seven-year-old daughter, Randy, and her six-year-old son, Matthew, waged an ear-piercing battle each evening about what program to watch on TV. Jane had tried everything to solve this daily problem—announcing that there would be no TV at all the next time she heard them arguing, sending both kids to their rooms to read in silence, drawing straws—all to no avail. One night's solution was quickly forgotten by the following evening. "I was so beside myself," Jane admitted, "that I started fantasizing about taking a BB gun, aiming it with sharpshooter accuracy, and simply blowing out the TV tube. I wondered, 'Am I going to have to listen to this every day for the rest of my life?' " Jane's children seemed completely oblivious to her growing distress. Fighting over the TV had become one of their favorite games.

One night, as the shrieking voices rose to a fever pitch from the den, Jane snapped. She marched into the room waving a full can of shaving cream and yelled at the top of her lungs, "Enough!" As her children paused and stared at her, Jane walked over and turned off the TV. Then, she vigorously shook the can of shaving cream and sprayed it all over the screen. "No more TV tonight," she announced.

The children's first reaction was speechless awe. Then they started giggling and soon they were rolling around on the floor. They thought it was the funniest thing they'd ever seen their mother do, and the humor of it distracted them from their argument. The fact that they couldn't watch TV that night hardly even mattered.

Wild and crazy reactions work wonders, as long as you don't use them too often. Liz found that being goofy helped get her eleven-year-old daughter's attention.

LIZ: I told you to clean up your room.
SAMANTHA: I'm busy.
LIZ: Samantha! I want it done now.
SAMANTHA: (defiantly) Stop bugging me about it.
LIZ: (now feeling infuriated) Do it now, or else!
SAMANTHA: Or else what?

"At that moment," Liz recalled, "my mind went completely blank. I wasn't prepared with an answer, and all the obvious threats seemed pointless. I blurted out the first thing that came to my mind, 'Or else I'll come up there and splatter purple paint all over your walls and on your clothes.'"

With a satisfied smile, Liz reported, "That stopped her. I think she was convinced that I had finally flipped my lid. Not only did she begin to clean up her room, she even laughed wryly, convinced that she really did have the nuttiest mother in her class."

Children love it when adults are silly, and it can be a good way to engage their cooperation. Humor helps release tension, and it can also give you a perspective about the absurdity of everyday battles.

🍂 *Don't take it personally.*

Priscilla, a parent whose youngest son frequently accused her of never saying yes to anything he wanted to do, decided that she was going to practice listening to her son's complaints, no matter how strongly he expressed them, without taking it personally. "Jeffrey has quite a mouth on him, as seven-year-olds do," she said. "Sometimes he would make antagonistic remarks and I wouldn't know how to react. I knew it was just kid's talk, but it was hard not to take it personally. I decided I was going to try a different method."

JEFFREY: You're a bad mother.

PRISCILLA: Oh, dear. Well, if you could take me back to the mommy shop, what would you ask them to fix?

JEFFREY: (now giggling) I would tell them to program you to always say yes when I wanted something, no matter what it was.

PRISCILLA: Goodness, you'd better start saving your allowance. That sounds like an expensive operation!

"Jeffrey loved to remind me from time to time that he was saving up his money so he could afford to send me to the mommy shop," Priscilla said. "It was amazing that when I didn't buy into the guilt, we actually turned Jeffrey's anger into a family joke."

Priscilla, without denying Jeffrey's words, responded by appealing to her child's fantasy of getting a more compliant mother. In doing so, she was letting him know that she understood his feelings, while gently suggesting a less negative way for him to express them.

Evelyn, a mother in one of my workshops, always spoke with warmth and pride about the close bond she felt with her son Rob. "My own parents were very critical," she said. "I could never tell them anything. But I made it safe for Rob to confide in me, and we enjoyed our time together. Then something dramatic happened. Puberty. I looked up one day and Rob's face was so full of disdain I couldn't believe it. Whenever I said anything, he'd respond by rolling his eyes or saying in a voice dripping with sarcasm, 'Oh, that's really brilliant, Mom—*not*.' What had I done to deserve such hostility? I was so upset, I called my mother who was continually telling me how thoughtful Rob was toward her. She laughed at my worries and reminded me that when I was Rob's age, I was so embarrassed by her that I always insisted on walking at least a block ahead of her on the street. Remembering my own feelings, I was able to see that Rob's behavior wasn't a personal attack on me."

❧ *Just laugh.*

Margaret, the mother of five children, related this dinnertime story. "At our evening meal, my husband and I sit at either end of the table, with two kids on each side and the baby's high chair next to me. One night our meal included green peas, not the kids' favorite vegetable, but we have a rule that they must eat at least some of their vegetable. I dished up each plate, ignoring the scrunched noses. For some reason, there wasn't the usual complaining about having to eat peas. The table was pretty quiet. I remember looking up once and noticing that the peas were disappearing from the kids' plates, and I thought, well, that's a surprise. Suddenly, the baby, sitting to my left, let out a huge wail. I looked, and there on his plate was a huge pile of peas. It seems that throughout dinner the kids had been slowly passing their peas down to the baby, hoping we wouldn't notice. Now, they were all looking very 'caught in the act,' wondering what we would do. To their surprise—and

somewhat to our own—my husband and I started laughing uproari-
ously. It was just so funny. No peas were eaten that night, but I'll bet
my kids will tell this story for years to come."

The wonderful thing about incidents like this one is that they become part of the uniting ritual of siblings. Decades later at family
gatherings, someone will say, "Remember the peas?" and it always
triggers laughter. Imagine how different the memory would be if the
parents had reacted by becoming furious and punishing the culprits. It
might then become an incident that nobody wanted to remember.

Obviously, it would be ludicrous to suggest that parents sit around
laughing merrily through the shattered glasses, misplaced retainers,
peanut butter prints on the new wallpaper, and chocolate syrup on the
rug. But most of us agree that a sense of humor is a very good quality.
In fact, we all want our children to acquire a sense of humor. So when
something is truly funny and no real damage has been done, the best
response may be the most obvious—just laugh.

❧ No excuses.

There's always a second chance, another day, an opportunity to do
something differently. If you really want to lighten up, you're going to
have to stop berating yourself when you mess up, or mulling over your
failures, or counting the number of times you think you blew it. Banish
the thought that you're a terrible parent, because if you really were a
terrible parent, you wouldn't be so upset. (And you certainly wouldn't
be reading this book!)

Be realistic. When you're sleep deprived or overworked, you can't
operate at your best—nobody can. At times like that, pat yourself on
the back if you can get through the day without major damage. Then
think about how you can find a way to take better care of yourself.
Remember, if you bury your own needs for the sake of the children, no
one wins. It's not easy. Sometimes you have to force yourself.

I remember a family vacation we took when Eric and Todd were
young. At the time, Todd was going through a very oppositional period.
We had booked two connecting rooms at the hotel, one for us and one

for the kids, and as soon as we arrived, Todd ran to examine each of the rooms. He was not pleased. "How come you and Dad get the best room?" he challenged me. I was very annoyed and about to give him my ten-minute lecture on entitlement. But I caught myself and replied instead, "Because we're the adults and we're paying." I felt a twinge of guilt, but Todd surprised me by accepting my answer with a shrug and saying, "Oh. Okay."

Had I been operating in my usual guilt mode, I probably would have tried to manufacture a long, well-reasoned explanation about why we needed more space and a better view, including the bit about telling Todd why he should be appreciative for all of the privileges we were providing. But in a rare moment, I slipped and told it like it was without apology, and guess what? It worked.

Parents often feel as though they don't have the right to place their needs before their children's. Michele was a mother in my workshop group who had elevated selfless devotion to a high art. We often encouraged her to find opportunities to assert her needs, and the occasion finally presented itself.

Michele was having one of those days from hell. Her four-year-old son, Matt, stepped in a bee's nest and got stung three times, the plumber came to fix the toilet, left to "get a part," and never returned, and the PTA called to remind her that she was on the list to supervise her daughter Judy's first-grade class trip, which was the following day. Although Michele always set aside forty-five minutes for talk and story time before her children went to bed, on this night, she canceled the nightly ritual, whisked the children off to bed crying tears of disappointment, while she fell into a guilty sleep.

The next morning she awoke and felt very rested. In the calm light of the morning, she regretted that she had skipped an important ritual the night before. But as she was sitting alone in the kitchen drinking her coffee and thinking about ways she could apologize and make things up to her children, she suddenly realized that this was a situation where she didn't have to make excuses. People get tired. She was tired. She deserved to go to bed early. Her children would not perish from lack of attention. Michele decided that she would not apologize to her children. She would try to use it as an opportunity to let them see her as a human being with needs. When they came down to breakfast, she engaged Matt and Judy in the following conversation:

MICHELE: Boy, I missed our story and talk time last night.

JUDY: So? Why didn't we do it?

MATT: Yeah, I didn't get to talk about my bee stings.

MICHELE: I was so tired last night I couldn't talk or read or listen. I just needed to sleep. You know how that is . . .

JUDY: You could have at least read us our stories.

MICHELE: Maybe. But I'm glad I didn't. It felt so wonderful to get under those blankets. I don't get very many chances to go to bed early, and I really enjoyed it. Thank you for being so quiet and not interrupting my precious sleep. This morning I woke up full of energy.

Michele told the group that her children didn't exactly respond with empathy and understanding. "But I didn't expect that," she said. "It would have been too much to ask them to agree that my needs were more important than theirs—especially since I've begun to realize that I haven't sent them that message often enough up until now. But at least I planted a seed that mommies have needs. It's a start." She beamed when every parent in the workshop gave her a round of applause.

Letting Go of the Angst

As I look back on the years when I was raising my sons, I sometimes regret that I wasn't lighter. I was such an earnest parent—always trying to teach and direct. I wore my ten-gallon parenting hat around every day, and its weight kept me solidly planted in the world of responsible adulthood. Now I wish I had been sillier and enjoyed their childish spontaneity more.

Where did we get the idea that in order to be good parents we have to be so serious? Our children can give us the best, most creative, funniest times we'll ever have. It's a shame to miss out on those times because we're too busy being diligent—especially since the so-called lessons we're usually trying to teach don't always take root.

Frieda, who was one of six children, remembered that her father always turned dinnertime into an educational lesson or contest. "The subjects varied from night to night," she said. "We'd do oceans of the world, state capitals, presidents, names of birds—whatever. I have no idea, because I never asked him, why he thought it was so important to do that every evening. But I suspect it was because he had no formal education beyond high school and worked at a low-paying job for most of his life. He valued education. I know my father meant well, but he was like a drill sergeant, and it was very unpleasant. I used to long for a meal when we just chatted and laughed and enjoyed our food. To this day, I can name all the state capitals, but I have a permanent intolerance for any and all rote learning. I'm sorry my father decided to use our dinner hour this way, because he missed the only chance he really had to just hang out and get to know us."

Humor and playfulness can soothe the most weary adult, serving as reminders that we're not just parenting machines, but real people. We want to enjoy life and have fun, too. When we open ourselves to the delightful aspects of having children, we are sometimes surprised to discover that the very things that drive us up the wall become transformed into the things that make having kids such a privilege. Kathryn, who used to complain bitterly about how stomach wrenching it could be to keep track of three very active young boys, had an eye-opening experience when she took her sons to the amusement park. "I remembered that when I was a child, I hated the merry-go-round because it was so boring, but I loved the thrill of the roller coaster. And suddenly it hit me: Being a parent was like the roller coaster, and that's what I really loved all along. Why did I keep wanting to make it like the merry-go-round?"

Chapter 10

Moments that Make It Worth It

If we dig them a hole,
   they'll fall into it;
If we build them a staircase,
   they'll climb it.

—a parent

Beverly knew she would always remember that moment. "It made an imprint on my mind and on my heart," she said when she telephoned to tell me about it. The incident occurred on a sunny morning in midsummer. Beverly was sitting at the kitchen table drinking coffee and reading the newspaper while Kim, six, and Brian, three, were playing in the backyard. Through the screen door, Beverly watched them out of the corner of her eye. "They weren't really playing together," Beverly said. "Kim usually tries to ignore Brian because he gets in her way. Brian is loud and boisterous. He's like a tank crashing around on the grass, while Kim is more reflective, gentle, and deliberate. She has lots of little yard treasures that she doesn't want Brian to touch—her shell collection, her seedlings, her bird feeders. Kim is happiest when she is in her little nature world, and Brian is happiest when he is squishing insects under foot, scaring away birds with his plastic water gun and interfering with Kim's projects. So as I sat in the kitchen, I had an ear cocked for the inevitable collision of their two worlds."

Kim and Brian had been playing in the backyard for twenty minutes without incident—a record for them—when suddenly Kim's voice came drifting through the screen door. Her tone made Beverly look up. "It was an unusual sound—patient, calm. The only way I can describe it is 'sisterly,' " Beverly said. "I went over to the door to see what was happening. Brian was sitting on the grass grinning with pure delight. Kim was kneeling beside him, her face pressed against his cheek. At first, I wasn't sure what she was doing, but then I realized she was giving Brian a 'butterfly kiss.' It's something I had taught her a couple of years ago. It involves pressing your eyelashes against the other person's cheek and fluttering them rapidly. The effect is a feather-light tickle. It's very loving. And now Kim was teaching her brother. I stood at the door for several minutes, mesmerized by the sight of my two children trading butterfly kisses."

As many parents have told me—and as I can attest from my own experience—sometimes all it takes is that small, often fleeting moment of siblings loving each other to erase the anxiety and anger that comes from their fighting and squabbling. Such moments may be all too rare, but when they do occur, they really have an impact, imprinting themselves on your memory to be recalled years later with pride and pleasure. These precious exchanges provide harassed parents with renewed optimism and remind them of the many reasons they had more than one child.

It's important to savor the lovely moments because so much of the time our heads are cluttered with the grittier realities. In fact, when I ask groups of parents to name the first thing that comes to mind when they hear the word "siblings," they respond without hesitation: "rivalry," followed by "fighting," "conflict," and "competition." I know that when Eric and Todd were young, I probably would have responded the same way. When you're in the thick of things, trying to juggle the needs of two or three or more children, the descriptions "loving," "devoted," "giggling," "loyal," and "tender" don't always come readily to mind. But occasionally, parents are surprised.

Harriet, the mother of two, told how a morning bus ride—ordinarily a chore—turned into an unexpected delight. "We have a subscription to the natural history museum children's magazine," Harriet said. "One day, as we were going out the door, the kids took the magazine along. On the bus there wasn't room for us to sit together, so I stayed in the front and they sat on the long seat in the back. From my distant seat, I watched them. They were huddled close together, showing each other pictures of penguins and whales and sharks. They were like two endearing little old men sitting and reading to each other in the back of the bus. I could see other people watching them, too—these charming children who loved each other and who would be together long after the rest of us were gone. Observing their total absorption in one another and their animated chatter was a special, unforgettable experience for me. I couldn't wait to get home and share it with my husband who usually hears nothing but my complaints about their fighting."

Elaine talked about sending her two children, ages nine and seven, to visit their grandparents in another state. It was to be the first time they were going on an airplane ride by themselves, and Elaine was feeling very edgy. "I was tired, the kids were jumping around, it took forever to maneuver through heavy traffic to the airport. When we finally arrived at the gate, Jonathan, the youngest, began to get very teary. Seeing that, I started to cry a little, too, and this made him even weepier. Missy was watching the two of us dissolve into tears, and suddenly she jumped up, took Jonathan's hand in hers and said in her brightest, most excited voice, 'I'm so happy, Jonny! I'm so happy to be going on the plane. Are you happy?' And a tender look came over his face, and he sniffed through his tears and said in a very small voice, 'Yes, I'm happy.' I was proud of Missy for seeing Jonathan's sadness and offering him comfort. She was sharing her happiness with him because he needed it. By the time they got on the plane, they were both smiling. I was the only one crying!"

Notice the Good Times

Margaret, a mother in one of my workshops, complained, "My kids are *always* fighting." It was a familiar refrain, an exaggerated perception that I hear all the time. I decided to do an experiment. "Take a pad," I suggested, "and for the next week make a check mark on it whenever your children are together and they're *not* fighting."

She agreed to try it, expecting the worst—an empty pad. But to her amazement, when she returned the following week, the pad was filled with many check marks.

"So, I guess your kids aren't always fighting?" I asked.

Margaret was a little embarrassed, but also very relieved. "The truth is, much of the time my kids aren't fighting. They're watching TV together or playing games. I think I just notice it more when they start to squabble because that's when they're raucous and they come running to me to complain. I must tell you, it was a big load off my mind to discover that my kids are friends as often as they are enemies."

Margaret's moment of insight was appreciated by other parents in the workshop. Soon everyone was relating examples of their kids being loving or giggling together or sharing secrets as siblings do.

The precious times when our children are enjoying one another or being loving, protective, and loyal can appear like unexpected gifts to harried parents. Suzanne, a mother who attended one of my workshops, was terribly disheartened by how nasty her twelve-year-old son, Eduardo, was toward his eight-year-old sister, Regina. "Regina adores Eduardo," Suzanne said, "but he constantly teases her and makes fun of her. He once told me that the best years of his life were the three and a half years before Regina was born. I was so upset, I wondered if it had been a mistake to have Regina. But the other day, I was looking out the window, and I saw Eduardo take Regina's hand in a very solicitous way as they were crossing the street. It seemed perfectly natural, and I'm sure he'd never do it if he knew I was watching. But I saw an intimate moment between them that I had never seen before. And the sheer naturalness of it convinced me that this protectiveness probably occurred often when they were out together. What a comfort."

"Yes, there are those moments," agreed Phyllis. "The other night, the four of us, my husband and I and both kids, were sitting in bed fooling around and having a tickling session, and everyone was laughing hysterically. It was so wonderful. I mean, sometimes my kids want to kill each other, but then there are times when I see them cracking up together over the most outrageous jokes, or goofing around, and it's the best feeling."

When all is said and done, what I have learned is this: No matter how stressed out, exhausted, and uncertain parents are, every person who has participated in my workshops or responded to my questionnaire has said they're very glad they have more than one child. If the pressures are greater, so, it seems, are the joys. "When you have only one child," said one mother, "you never hear the squabbling, the angry scenes, the complaining, or the jealousy. But you also never have the experience of hearing your kids giggling together, telling secrets, sticking up for each other, or plotting together."

These are the times we need to savor and treasure. They fill us with the intense pleasure of having more than one. They give us joy in the moment, and memories that we can call to mind to comfort us during the hard times.

What parents start to realize, when they are encouraged to gain some perspective, is that being in a family is chaotic and muddled, just like life. And like life, there are the painful, disappointing moments, and also those which are uplifting, that sustain us and make it all worthwhile.

Elizabeth, whose sons, ages five and three and a half, were locked in a noisy rivalry that made her despair of ever seeing a loving moment between them, was surprised when her elder son approached her one day with a strange question. "He asked, 'Mom, when Jeffrey and I were born, were we hugging each other?' I was momentarily flabbergasted by the question," Elizabeth said. "Finally, I reminded him that he had been born first—almost three years before his brother. I asked him if he remembered that time before his brother was born. By the look on his face, I realized that he didn't. In his mind, they were a pair and always had been."

Parents also agree that in spite of the extra challenges, it's better for their children to have each other. It forces them to learn to share and care, to think of someone else's needs, to compromise and apologize and to be concerned social beings in a world that won't always put them first. Parents strongly believe that this is the essence of what it means to be a family—the heart of what made them decide to have more than one child in the first place.

Every so often, the kids themselves reveal a compassionate side that almost makes the fights seem worth it. One parent shared this note, written by eighteen-year-old Molly to her thirteen-year-old sister, Alissa, following a bitter fight over the computer.

Dear Alissa,

I want to say that I am truly sorry for most of what I said last night. Sometimes when I am angry I lash out and say what I know is most hurtful.

I do know that you work very hard. I had no right to say otherwise. I also understand how it feels to always have someone borrowing something that is yours. You "deserve" that computer merely because you are a wonderful person. I just get angry because I am frustrated and would like to use it as well.

Sometimes when you are in a bad mood I feel as if you are distancing yourself from me and pushing me away instead of confiding in me and letting me be on your side. I feel hurt but I must realize that you like to deal with your problems on your own.

Just understand that you can always come to me for help or a shoulder to cry on. I love you very much.

Molly

Parents of more than one find themselves challenged daily, and I am struck by how remarkably well so many of them rise to this challenge. They discover coping skills they never knew they had, find strength and creativity beyond what they thought they were capable of. In moments of reflection, they define this as one of the rewarding aspects of being parents to more than one child.

"When I had my first, I couldn't imagine ever loving another child," a mother told me. "Joey was the center of my universe. Then, when Ellen came along, I was astonished by how easily my love stretched to include her. I'm glad I had a second child because I was so intensely wrapped up with Joey that it was just too much—for him and for me. We're more balanced now and happier."

A Glimpse of the Future

There's no way to know what the future will bring, but that doesn't stop us from worrying about it. As I talk to parents of siblings, I find that they spend a lot of time wondering and hoping that their children will be better off for having siblings, but they're often filled with nagging doubts. Will their kids love each other and be close as adults? Will they harbor lifelong resentments? Will they be embattled or supportive? Will family gatherings be warm, delightful occasions or will they be tense and factionalized?

Evelyn, the mother of four children now grown, sometimes attends my workshops to get tips for her new job of grandparenting. The other parents always love having her there because she is such an unwavering voice of optimism. With the wisdom of time and experience, Evelyn is able to say, "The camaraderie my children eventually developed as they got older has been the best part of having more than one child. Mind you, there were times when I would never have envisioned it happening, but it has. It gives me tremendous joy to feel their love."

Evelyn supplied this example of a particularly poignant moment. "It happened on my daughter Kathleen's twenty-third birthday," she said. "First, a bit of background. On Kathleen's fifth birthday, we had given her a big, cuddly Raggedy Ann doll—the original kind with the red 'I Love You' heart on its chest. Kathleen adored this doll, carried it with her, talked to it, and slept with it. Her two brothers, then nine and seven, liked to tease Kathleen about her doll. They thought the 'I Love

You' heart was especially corny. One day Kathleen came running to me shrieking and sobbing, holding the doll, whose heart had been mutilated with red Magic Marker. The 'I Love You' was crossed out, replaced by the words 'I Hate You.' We all knew it was the work of her brothers, and they even admitted it. They thought it was soooo funny, and it made me sad that they could take such delight in their sister's misery. From that day onward, Kathleen never played with her Raggedy Ann again. In the years to come, she would often mention the incident as the worst thing her brothers ever did. So now, on her twenty-third birthday, her brothers arrived at the house with a very large box. Inside was a giant-size Raggedy Ann and a note from her brothers that read: 'Sorry about your doll. Better late than never.' It was very funny and very moving all at once. For me, it was the perfect example of the way my children have grown to cherish each other."

I can relate to Evelyn's pleasure. As I look back on the years when my sons were young, I am sometimes amazed to remember how disheartened I was by their unwillingness to cooperate and share and be kind to one another. Yet here they are today, the best of friends and the closest of confidants. When they get together after they've been separated for a while, they greet each other with enthusiastic hugs and squeezes, and hearty cries of "Hi, bro!" They barely manage to greet us before they go off together and spend hours trading stories, jokes, and (I am sure) private observations about their parents, whom they affectionately call "The Rents."

When I was doing research for this book, I asked parents to think back to the conflicts they had with their brothers and sisters when they were children. I wondered if those conflicts were left behind with maturity, or if they still remained. I knew it was every parent's worst fear—that the rivalry would last forever and perhaps grow worse. Most people reported that their adult relationships with their siblings were complicated. They couldn't answer my question by saying yes, the rivalry was still there, or no, it wasn't. In fact, many people answered quite frankly that they still struggled with their siblings. Personalities still clashed; old questions of favoritism still lingered.

This may be a somewhat uncomfortable truth—and not one that

worried parents want to hear. Yet I have found that even when conflicts remain, the sibling bond is somehow transcendent. Your siblings are irreplaceable and unique among your relationships. They may never be your closest friends, but their role is more enduring than any friendship. They are the continuity of your life, a part of your history. You can't divorce them, and even if your relationship is not perfect, you wouldn't want to. Love them or not, they are and always will be part of you.

I was reminded of this fact in a very painful way four years ago when my brother, Tom, died of cancer. Tom was a vigorous, energetic, and playful man who was cut down in his prime. He was so full of life and had so much more living to do, but it was not to be. During his illness and after his death, I had many opportunities to reflect about what our relationship had been. When we were kids, we had been combative—I loved to tease him and he loved to beat me up. As adults, Tom and I didn't have much in common, and we lived on opposite coasts. And yet, we understood things about each other and could summon up our joint recollections easily. I realized that in losing Tom I lost a piece of my history. He was the only witness to many events in my life, the only one who could savor certain hilarious memories from our childhood. Never again could I tease him with the recollection, "Remember the time after the senior prom when you got so drunk that you raided the refrigerator and ate a piece of raw chicken?" There would be no more laughing over the old absurdities.

Tom's death left me feeling angry and profoundly sad. It seemed so unfair that such an exuberant man with so many good and loyal friends and such a deep love of life could be gone. Yet, unexpectedly, his illness provided a precious opportunity for us to experience our relationship in a new way. We spent more time together during Tom's last five months than we had for years. It was horrible for me to watch my robust brother become thin and fragile and begin to waste away. But my respect and admiration for him grew with each visit. During his decline, Tom rarely complained, and he radiated a certain serenity and gentleness I had never seen in him before. Now, when I think of Tom, I have a new memory—of his great courage during the final months.

My sister, Ellen, is ten years younger than I, and although we have different fathers, we have much in common. We share an interest in maintaining traditions and keeping the family together, and this is one of our strongest bonds. Over the years, as adults, Ellen and I have faced a number of difficult issues, and some of them remain unresolved. Our relationship is very much a work in progress, but that doesn't preclude enjoyment and satisfaction. For example, I love the way we can communicate an entire chapter of history with a raised eyebrow or a knowing grin. All one of us has to do is say the word "Fifi," and we are reminded of how we shared a deep envy of our mother's beloved poodle—a four-legged "perfect child" who was always affectionate and could do no wrong. Recently, Ellen remarried and invited me to be her matron of honor. I felt very close to her that day, and delighted in how happy she was and how lovely she looked. It was one of those unforgettable times when the spoken and unspoken conflicts that remain between us were completely eclipsed by my pride and pleasure.

The sibling bond, as I experienced it with my brother and sister, and have heard it described by others, is a mysterious mix of the silly and the profound. It is a bond forged by daily life, pieced together with incidents that mean nothing to anyone but the siblings themselves. If all things are equal, your sibling relationship will constitute the longest of your life—and it was certainly the earliest. Your brothers and sisters were the ones who knew you before you crafted your public face; they were around for the messy business of growing up. Most of the other people who know you today probably came along after you learned to use a fork and knife and toilet, after you learned to tie your shoes, after you learned to read and speak in complete sentences, after your manners had evolved. Most of your adult friends probably didn't know you when your idea of fun was hiding a worm in your brother's sock or embarrassing your sister by making loud smooching sounds when her first date came to the door. They weren't privy to your teenage humiliations and the immature acts you'd rather forget. But your siblings are special and unique. They were there as witnesses. They knew you when!

Appendix A

Reading List

WELCOMING NUMBER TWO/DEALING WITH TODDLERS AND PRESCHOOLERS:

Eisenberg, Murkoff, and Hathaway. *What to Expect: The Toddler Years.* New York: Workman, 1994.

Galinsky, Ellen, and Judy David. *The Preschool Years.* New York: Times Books, 1988.

Lansky, Vicki. *Welcoming Your Second Baby.* Deephaven, MN: Book Peddlers, 1990.

Lieberman, Alicia. *The Emotional Life of the Toddler.* New York: Free Press, 1995.

Miller, Karen. *Things to Do with Toddlers and Twos.* Chelsea, MA: Telshare Publishing, 1984.

WORKING PARENTS/STRESS:

Balter, Lawrence. *Not in Front of the Children: How to Talk to Your Children About Tough Family Matters.* New York: Penguin, 1994.

Brazelton, T. Berry. *Working and Caring.* Reading, MA: Addison-Wesley, 1987.

Pillsbury, Linda G. *Survival Tips for Working Moms: 297 Real Tips from Real Moms.* Los Angeles: Perspective Publishing, 1994.

Siegler, Ava. *What Should I Tell the Kids? A Parent's Guide to Real Problems in the Real World.* New York: Dutton, 1993.

SIBLING RIVALRY/SIBLING RELATIONSHIPS:

Ames, Louise Bates. *He Hit Me First: When Brothers and Sisters Fight.* New York: Warner, 1989.

Bank, Stephen, and Michael Kahn. *The Sibling Bond.* New York: Basic Books, 1982.

Calladine, Andrew and Carole. *Raising Brothers and Sisters without Raising the Roof.* Minneapolis: Winston Press, 1990.

Faber, Adele, and Elaine Mazlish. *Siblings without Rivalry.* New York: Avon, 1987.

Hapworth, William and Mada, and Joan Heilman. *Mom Loved You Best.* New York: Penguin, 1994.

Klagsbrun, Francine. *Mixed Feelings: Love, Hate, Rivalry, and Reconciliation Among Brothers and Sisters.* New York: Bantam, 1992.

Mathias, Barbara. *Between Sisters: Secret Rivals, Intimate Friends.* New York: Delacorte, 1992.

Reit, Seymour. *Sibling Rivalry.* New York: Ballantine, 1985.

Weiss, Joan Solomon. *Your Second Child: A Guide for Parents.* New York: Summit Books, 1981.

PARENTS TOGETHER OR APART:

Blau, Melinda. *Families Apart: Ten Keys to Successful Co-parenting.* New York: Putnam, 1993.

Kennedy, Marge, and Janet Spencer King. *The Single Parent Family: Living Happily in a Changing World.* New York: Crown, 1994.

Krueger, Caryl. *Single with Children.* Nashville, TN: Abingdon Press, 1993.

Lansky, Vicki. *Vicki Lansky's Divorce Book for Parents.* New York: New American Library, 1989.

Miller, Naomi. *Single Parents by Choice: A Growing Trend in Family Life.* New York: Plenum Press, 1992.

Taffel, Ron. *Why Parents Disagree: How Women and Men Parent Differently and How We Can Work Together.* New York: William Morrow, 1994.

Visher, John and Emily. *How to Win as a Stepfamily.* Chicago: Contemporary Books, 1982.

Wallerstein, Judith, and Joan Kelly. *Surviving the Breakup: How Parents and Children Cope with Divorce.* New York: HarperCollins, 1990.

CHALLENGING CHILDREN/SPECIAL NEEDS:

Albrecht, Donna G. *Raising a Child Who Has a Physical Disability.* New York: John Wiley, 1995.

Hallowell, Edward, and John Ratey. *Driven to Distraction: Recognizing and Coping with ADD from Childhood Through Adulthood.* New York: Touchstone, 1995.

Kurcinka, Mary S. *Raising Your Spirited Child.* New York: HarperPerennial, 1992.

Osman, Betty. *Learning Disabilities: A Family Affair.* New York: Random House, 1979.

———. *No One to Play With: The Social Side of Learning Disabilities.* New York: Warner, 1980.

Turecki, Stanley. *The Difficult Child.* New York: Bantam, 1985.

———. *Normal Children Have Problems, Too.* New York: Bantam, 1995.

Tuttle, Cheryl, and Penny Paquette. *Parenting a Child with Learning Disabilities.* New York: Doubleday, 1995.

Wylie, Betty Jane. *The Book of Matthew.* New York: S.P.I. Books, 1984.

PRACTICAL PARENTING/ENCOURAGING COOPERATION:

Cline, Foster, and Jim Fay. *Parenting with Love and Logic: Teaching Children Responsibility.* Colorado Springs, CO: Piñon Press, 1990.

Coloroso, Barbara. *Kids Are Worth It: Giving Your Child the Gift of Inner Discipline.* New York: William Morrow, 1994.

Crary, Elizabeth. *Kids Can Cooperate: A Practical Guide to Teaching Problem Solving.* Seattle, WA: Parenting Press, 1985.

Faber, Adele, and Elaine Mazlish. *How to Talk So Kids Will Listen, and Listen So Kids Will Talk.* New York: Avon, 1982.

Ginott, Haim. *Between Parent and Child.* New York: Avon, 1965.

Kutner, Lawrence. *Parent and Child: Getting Through to Each Other.* New York: Avon, 1992.

Le Shan, Eda. *When Your Child Drives You Crazy.* New York: St. Martin's, 1986.

Nelsen, Jane, Lynn Lott, and H. Stephen Glenn. *Positive Discipline A–Z: 1001 Solutions to Everyday Parenting Problems.* Rocklin, CA: Prima Publishing, 1993.

Samalin, Nancy. *Love and Anger: The Parental Dilemma.* New York: Penguin, 1991.

———. *Loving Your Child Is Not Enough: Positive Discipline That Works.* New York: Penguin, 1988.

Shure, Myrna. *Raising a Thinking Child.* New York: Henry Holt, 1994.

Tempelsman, Cathy. *Child-Wise.* New York: William Morrow, 1995.

Weinhaus, Evonne, and Karen Friedman. *Stop Struggling with Your Child.* New York: HarperPerennial, 1991.

FATHERING:

Marzollo, Jean. *Fathers and Toddlers: How Toddlers Grow and What They Need from You from 18 Months to Three Years.* New York: Harper Perennial, 1994.

Scull, Charles. *Fathers, Sons, and Daughters: Exploring Fatherhood, Renewing the Bond.* New York: Jeremy P. Tarcher/Perigee, 1992.

Shapiro, Jerrold. *The Measure of a Man: Becoming the Man You Wish Your Father Was.* New York: Delacorte, 1993.

Sullivan, S. Adams. *The Father's Almanac,* rev. ed. New York: Doubleday, 1992.

TWINS/MULTIPLES:

Bryan, Elizabeth. *Twins, Triplets, and More: From Pre-birth Through High School.* New York: St. Martin's, 1992.

Friedrich, Elizabeth. *The Parent's Guide to Raising Twins.* New York: St. Martin's, 1990.

Novotny, Pamela. *The Joy of Twins and Multiples.* New York: Crown, 1994.

Rothbart, Betty. *Multiple Blessings.* New York: Hearst Books, 1994.

ADOPTION:

Krementz, Jill. *How It Feels to Be Adopted.* New York: Knopf, 1982.

Melina, Lois R. *Making Sense of Adoption: A Parent's Guide.* New York: Harper & Row, 1989.

Schaffer, Judith, and Christina Lindstrom. *How to Raise an Adopted Child.* New York: Plume, 1991.

BUILDING SELF-ESTEEM:

Bingham, Mindy, and Sandy Stryker. *Things Will Be Different for My Daughter: A Practical Guide to Building Her Self-Esteem and Self-Reliance.* New York: Penguin, 1995.

Hart, Louise. *The Winning Family: Increasing Self-Esteem in Your Children and Yourself.* Oakland, CA: LifeSkills Press, 1990.

Kurshan, Neil. *Raising Your Child to Be a Mensch.* New York: Ballantine, 1989.

Lansky, Vicki. *101 Ways to Make Your Child Feel Special.* Chicago: Contemporary Books, 1991.

Phillips, Debora. *How to Give Your Child a Great Self-Image.* New York: Plume, 1989.

ADOLESCENT ISSUES:

Caron, Ann. *Don't Stop Loving Me: A Reassuring Guide for Mothers of Adolescent Daughters.* New York: HarperCollins, 1992.

————. *Strong Mothers, Strong Sons: Raising Adolescent Boys in the '90s.* New York: HarperCollins, 1995.

Ginott, Haim. *Between Parent and Teenager.* New York: Avon, 1969.

Pipher, Mary. *Reviving Ophelia: Saving the Selves of Adolescent Girls.* New York: Ballantine, 1994.

Warren, Andrea, and Jay Weidenkeller. *Everybody's Doing It.* New York: Penguin, 1993.

Wolf, Anthony. *Get Out of My Life but First Could You Drive Me and Cheryl to the Mall?* New York: Noonday Press, 1991.

THE LIGHTER SIDE:

Hickey, Mary, and Sandra Salmans. *The Working Mother's Guilt Guide.* New York: Penguin, 1992.

Lansky, Bruce. *Mother Murphy's Law and Other Perils of Parenthood.* Deephaven, MN: Meadowbrook Press, 1986.

Sunshine, Linda. *"Mom Loves Me Best" (and Other Lies You Told Your Sister).* New York: NAL/Dutton, 1990.

GENERAL PARENTING/ADVICE:

Quindlen, Anna. *Living Out Loud.* New York: Random House, 1988.

Satir, Virginia. *The New Peoplemaking.* Palo Alto, CA: Science and Behavior Books, 1988.

Swigart, Jane. *The Myth of the Bad Mother.* New York: Avon, 1992.

Trelease, Jim. *The New Read-Aloud Handbook,* 4th edition (revised). New York: Penguin, 1989.

Appendix B

Here is the parents' questionnaire that was so instrumental in researching this book.

1. Do you yourself have siblings? If so, list their sex and ages.

SEX   AGE

_____ _____

_____ _____

_____ _____

You are number _____ in the lineup.

2. Recall the ways your parents handled you and your siblings. For example:

- Did they intervene when you fought, or let you work things out on your own?
- Did they have special ways of making things seem fair, or did you often feel that there was an imbalance?

- Did they tend to treat you as a group (i.e., "the kids," "the girls") or did they find ways to make you feel special or unique?

Please elaborate on these or other memories from your childhood.

3. Do you find yourself using methods similar to those your parents used? If so, describe which of your methods are the same. If you handle your children very differently from your parents, please elaborate.

4. Do you think your mother or father had a "favorite" child? If so, how was this manifested? Were there things that were said or behaviors that convinced you of this favoritism? How did you or your siblings relate to the child who was perceived to be the favorite?

5. Do you now find that the things that annoyed you about your sibling(s) when you were young still bother you? Describe how your relationship changed as you matured. (For example, one woman recalled how envious and competitive she and her sister were as children, but how they have now become allies in dealing with their aging parents.)

6. Were you an only child? If so, did that factor influence you to have more than one child? Please elaborate.

7. Your own children are:

FIRST NAME	SEX	AGE
_____	_____	_____
_____	_____	_____
_____	_____	_____
_____	_____	_____
_____	_____	_____
_____	_____	_____

8. Describe the reaction of your first child to having a new baby in the house. Also, comment on the ways you prepared your child for the arrival of a new sibling.

9. The first year is very different from other years. How did your older child's reaction to his/her sibling change as the second child outgrew infancy?

• How did your second child deal with being younger or the youngest?

• If you have three or more children, how did subsequent children deal with being older or younger? Did you see any evidence of a "middle child syndrome"? If so, please describe.

10. Do you and your spouse both work outside the home? If so, how have you managed to balance the demands of having two or more children?

11. Are there particular areas of conflict between you and your spouse about raising more than one child—such as favoritism or gender preferences? Please elaborate.

12. Does your family include stepchildren or half siblings? If so, give examples of particular issues that get raised in your household that are unique to these relationships.

13. What would you describe as the advantages of having more than one child?

14. What would you describe as the disadvantages of having more than one child?

15. Do you have a child with health or other problems who requires special attention? If so, describe your circumstances and how you deal with sibling issues that arise as a result.

16. It's normal to sometimes prefer one child over another—often because that child is easier to handle. Does one or more of your children tend to get along better with you or your spouse? If and when you find yourself or your spouse favoring one of your children, how do you deal with it?

17. What do your children fight about?

18. Do your kids often say, "It's not fair," or "You love her [him] more"? How do you respond when this happens?

19. What specific solutions have you discovered that resolve conflicts, ease the rivalry, enhance the relationships—or address other sibling issues? In particular, what methods have you found helpful in enabling your children to get along—and at what ages have they worked best?

20. Are there particular issues that you, as the parent of more than one child, would like to see addressed in this book? What would you find most helpful?

Appendix C

This is the children's survey I used that shed so much light on how siblings really feel about each other.

1. How do you feel about having brothers and sisters?

2. Do you ever wish you were an only child?

3. What do you fight about?

4. Do you fight more when your parents are around or when they're not?

5. Do you ever deliberately hurt each other, emotionally or physically?

6. Do you ever tattle to get a sibling in trouble? What happens when you do?

7. Do you make up fast or does it take a while?

8. When you're upset or having a problem, do you talk to your siblings or your parents or both? Who is the most helpful?

9. Do your parents play favorites or take sides?

10. Do you wish your parents would intervene more than they do, or do they intervene too often?

11. Do you and your siblings share secrets together?

12. Do you sometimes stick up for each other or take sides together against your parents or friends?

13. Do you have stepbrothers or sisters? How is your relationship with them different than the one with your siblings by birth? The same?

14. What is the worst part of having siblings?

15. What's the best part of having siblings?

16. When you're grown and have a family, would you have more than one child? If so, why?

Index

About the Author

❧

Nancy Samalin is a nationally renowned parenting expert whose widely acclaimed books *Love and Anger: The Parental Dilemma* (winner of the *Child* Magazine Award for Best Parenting Book of 1991) and *Loving Your Child Is Not Enough* have been a source of enormous comfort to countless parents. Ms. Samalin is a consulting editor and columnist for *Parents* magazine. As founder and director of Parent Guidance Workshops, she has been conducting workshops for parents for two decades, and lectures throughout the U.S. and abroad. She is on the adjunct faculty of Bank Street College of Education, where she received her master's degree and professional diploma in counseling.

AUTHOR'S NOTE:

I am eager to hear from you, and welcome your comments, reactions, and suggestions. Let me know what worked for you and what difficulties you may have encountered. Should you wish to contact me for information about lectures, workshops, and speaking engagements, please write to me in care of

Bantam Books
1540 Broadway
New York, NY 10036

or fax me directly at PARENT GUIDANCE WORKSHOPS (212) 787-9029.